PRAISE FOR *HOW TO BE FREE*

"Shaka's journey is a powerful testament to the transformative power of self-discovery and resilience. During his years in solitary confinement, he was able to break through his internal barriers and emerge with a powerful sense of purpose that enabled him to make a massive impact on the world. This inspiring read is a must for anyone committed to personal growth, leadership, and creating lasting change."
—Reid Hoffman, cofounder of LinkedIn and *New York Times* bestselling author of *Superagency*

"Senghor's fearless self-reflection serves as a guidebook for anyone.... His lessons resonate in every walk of life, from the streets to the boardroom."
—Mellody Hobson, president of Ariel Investments

"With deft storytelling and raw emotion, Senghor proves, once more, that the most ordinary of us can become extraordinary when we choose courage and conviction in the face of unimaginable grief."
—Joanne Molinaro, creator of *The Korean Vegan* and *New York Times* bestselling author

"Real freedom is not having unlimited choices but rather living a life of purpose that empowers others to be who they can be. Shaka Senghor shares with us what he learned after a lifetime of adversity and decades of imprisonment: Freedom isn't the ability to do whatever you want—it's an internal decision to be grateful and present in all circumstances."
—Jim Murphy, *New York Times* bestselling author of *Inner Excellence*

"The philosophers of our time who matter most are those whose insights spring from gritty, lived experience, not classroom musings. I call them 'street philosophers.' And I believe Shaka is one of the greats, a modern wise elder. This book is a gift, revealing layers of Shaka's wisdom, and belongs on bedside tables and kitchen tables to be read time and again for its authentic insights and virtuous guidance."
—Brad Keywell, 2019 EY World Entrepreneur of the Year, founder of nine technology companies, creator of Chicago Ideas and WNDR Museum

HOW TO BE FREE

Also by Shaka Senghor

Writing My Wrongs: Life, Death, and Redemption in an American Prison

Letters to the Sons of Society: A Father's Invitation to Love, Honesty, and Freedom

Composure: The Art of Keeping It Together

HOW TO BE FREE

A PROVEN GUIDE TO ESCAPING LIFE'S HIDDEN PRISONS

SHAKA SENGHOR

NEW YORK TIMES BESTSELLING AUTHOR
AND RESILIENCE EXPERT

Authors Equity
1123 Broadway, Suite 1008
New York, New York 10010

Copyright © 2025 by Shaka Senghor
All rights reserved.

Cover design by Pete Garceau
Book design by Scribe Inc.

Most Authors Equity books are available at a discount when purchased in quantity for sales promotions or corporate use. Special editions, which include personalized covers, excerpts, and corporate imprints, can be created when purchased in large quantities. For more information, please email info@authorsequity.com.

Library of Congress Control Number: 2025937193
Print ISBN 9798893310511
Ebook ISBN 9798893310535

Printed in the United States of America
First printing

www.authorsequity.com

When I first sat down to write this dedication, the obvious names came to mind—my wife, my sons, my parents. The people who have stood by me, loved me, and believed in me. But then it hit me:

This one is for me.

This book brought me joy. It helped me confront and uproot my own hidden prisons. It reminded me that I'm worthy—not just of love and success but of honoring my own journey. So I dedicate this body of work to every version of myself who made it here.

To the little boy they called Pumpkin.

To the broken teenager the streets renamed Jay.

To the young man, James White, who walked into a prison cell at nineteen.

And to the man, Shaka Senghor, who has carried them all into the light.

I've survived everything thrown my way. I've outlasted trauma, quieted self-doubt, and stared fear in the face. I've earned this peace. I've earned this joy. I've earned the right to thrive.

So here's to you, Big Dog—for a job well done and a fight well won.

In memoriam

Sherrod Redd, Charles Oneal, and Indyego (Indy)

Author's Note

The events described in this book really happened. However, to protect the privacy of certain individuals, some names, identifying characteristics, and personal details have been altered.

Contents

Preface xiii

Introduction xvii

How to Use This Book xxiii

PART 1 BREAKING THE CHAINS

1 Grief 3

2 Anger 27

3 Shame 48

PART 2 FINDING YOUR STRENGTH

4 Vulnerability 69

5 Forgiveness 86

6 Resilience 100

CONTENTS

PART 3 **EMBRACING FREEDOM**

7 Hope and Composure   125

8 Love   142

9 Joy   158

10 Success   170

11 Facing Down Fear   183

12 Becoming Unstoppable   192

13 Finding True Freedom   205

Recommendations   225

Acknowledgments   229

About the Author   235

> You want to fly, you got to give up the shit that weighs you down.
>
> —Toni Morrison, *Song of Solomon*

Preface

I was born in Detroit, Michigan, in 1972.

By the time I was a teenager, the streets had become my classroom. Violence was normal. Fear was constant. And in 1991, at nineteen years old, I made a decision that would change my life forever.

I shot and killed a man.

For that, I was sentenced to seventeen to forty years in prison. I ended up serving nineteen—seven of them in solitary confinement.

Prison is designed to break you. The walls, the rules, the routine—it's all meant to strip you down until you forget who you are. But what I discovered is that the most powerful prisons aren't the ones made of concrete and steel. They're the ones we carry with us—built from grief, anger, shame, trauma, and self-doubt. The ones that keep us stuck, even when the door is wide open.

And here's what I've learned: Prisons have doors. And those doors can be opened.

I walked out of prison in 2010 into a world where people like me were expected to fail. Where 67.8 percent of men who had served time would be back behind bars within three years. But I refused to be a statistic. Instead, I became a student of freedom—not just physical freedom but mental, emotional, and spiritual freedom.

What I learned inside those walls wasn't just how to survive—I learned how to rebuild, adapt, and overcome. And over the years, I've developed a deep understanding of resilience—not just as an idea but as a practice.

Today, I teach that practice to others. Executives, founders, athletes, and world-class leaders come to me—not because they've been to prison but because they feel trapped.

Some are battling impostor syndrome, questioning whether they truly belong in the rooms in which they've earned a seat. Some are entrepreneurs frozen by self-doubt, afraid to take the risks that lead to success. Others are parents trapped by perfectionism, struggling under the weight of expectations.

And that's when I remind them of the truth:

Everyone has hidden prisons. But every prison has a door.

As a resilience expert, my work is rooted in helping people break free—whether from past mistakes, limiting beliefs, or self-imposed barriers. Over the years, I've developed a framework that has helped leaders, creators, and innovators build lives of clarity, purpose, and impact.

This book is about that framework.

Freedom isn't a destination I reached when I walked out of prison—it's a path I continue to walk every day. What I've learned is that freedom requires constant renewal. Just when you think you've found it, life can shake you to your core, and suddenly

PREFACE

those invisible restraints tighten again. The journey I share along with the techniques for reclaiming freedom speak to a universal truth: liberation is a practice we must recommit to daily, especially in our most challenging moments.

Through raw storytelling and hard-won experience, I'll show you how to design your own freedom ecosystem—using strategic mindfulness, emotional regulation, and purposeful boundary setting to break free from whatever is holding you back. These aren't abstract theories. They're battle-tested tools, forged in the hardest conditions imaginable.

One of my core mantras is simple but powerful:

"I don't have to wait to be free. I am free right now. I am free from the weight of my past. I don't owe my old mistakes my future."

This is not just another personal development book. It's a blueprint—a guide for anyone ready to step into the life they were meant to live.

Let's get free.

Introduction

> He who is not courageous enough to take risks will accomplish nothing in life.
>
> —Muhammad Ali

The words "Parole Denied" sat at the top of the paper I held in my hand, mocking me with this second denial. Sitting on the edge of my bunk, my perch for eighteen years, I was caught in what felt like an endless loop of confinement and disappointment. I had grown up here, transformed from rebel to writer, witnessed some friends die, some lose their mental grip, and others leave and come back. Would they ever let me out of this place?

My body tensed as I held back tears. Emotions rolled through me in waves—sadness flowing into the familiarity of anger, the kind that threatened to overtake the little hope I had left. I had ticked every box, followed the Department of Corrections' criteria for release, and evolved in ways no one would have imagined possible. In my first five years there, I had been labeled the worst of the worst, but now I was a mentor, tutor, and writer. Back at square one, it was like being sentenced all over again.

INTRODUCTION

But as I sat there, enveloped in the familiar hurricane of disappointment, a realization slowly dawned on me: I had a choice. This moment, as heartbreaking as it was, presented me with two options. I could succumb to depression, let it drag me down into that dark place of hopelessness from which there seemed no escape, or I could stand firm on the hope that had already carried me over many troubled waters and use this setback as an opportunity to prepare myself for the next hearing and, ultimately, for my freedom.

As Marcus Aurelius wrote in *Meditations*, "The impediment to action advances action. What stands in the way becomes the way." This perfectly captured the transformative work I'd been engaged in for years—the work of freeing the mind, body, and soul. It was work that challenged me to embrace the present moment as both a gift and an opportunity. It's work we all have the capacity to do.

My parole denial was an obstacle to my freedom, but within that moment lay the path forward.

I came out of that moment with renewed focus and determination. When the yard opened, I called my dad and broke the news to him. Then I walked the yard with a friend from the neighborhood and talked about what I was going to do when they released me.

When the third parole hearing finally arrived, I stood before the board not just as a man seeking freedom but as one who had already freed himself internally. I was battered and bruised but still standing. The moment I received the paperwork stamped "Parole Granted," it was not just a release from physical

INTRODUCTION

confinement but a validation and manifestation of the journey I had undertaken. It was finally time for me to return to my city, community, and family. In that moment, I realized I'd been in prison before I'd ever been arrested and that I'd broken free long before the parole board saw fit to release me.

I had defied the odds, narrowly escaping the expected outcome of a kid serving a seventeen- to forty-year sentence for murder. It had been two decades since I'd last walked on free soil, unburdened by handcuffs and shackles. Despite scars from an officer nearly breaking my arm, an unhealed anterior cruciate ligament (ACL) tear from another encounter, and a bad back, my sanity, spiritual well-being, and integrity remained largely intact. Still, I struggled with feelings of self-doubt and worthlessness—vulnerabilities that could have been imperiled by release.

As I write, that was fifteen years ago, and the battle with those imprisoning voices has been a long war. Freedom isn't just a paper stamped by the parole board—it's a gift we unwrap every day through our choices and actions.

Today, through my work as an author, speaker, and entrepreneur—things I dreamed about both during my incarceration and after my release—I have met countless individuals grappling with their own relentless inner and outer imprisoning voices: prisons of grief, anger, shame, and the inability to forgive. At book signings, after keynote speeches or fireside chats, people share how my story helped them get through a divorce, get over the suicide of a child, or take the next step in their career—people of every race, creed, and gender expressing deep gratitude for

INTRODUCTION

being released from something that was holding them back. Regardless of our individual journeys, survivor's remorse, trauma, and guilt are common struggles that stand in the way of becoming the individuals we aspire to be. Everyone has a hidden prison.

That's precisely why I wanted to write this book—to offer skills that can help people break free from the emotional, psychological, and metaphorical prisons, both seen and unseen, that confine them. While some of us have experienced physical incarceration, many others find themselves trapped by circumstances, serving time handed down from a difficult childhood, horrible work experiences, heartbreak, and traumatic events or confined behind invisible bars that exist in their minds.

Now, as I sit here in my office, I look at my life, the people I love, the experiences I am blessed to have, and the way I move through the world with presence and awareness, and I feel my heart aligning with something greater: love, joy, purpose, and healing, for myself and for others. I have finally become all the things I once imagined myself to be years ago: an artist, an entrepreneur, a father, and a husband. My only concern now is fighting for the deeper parts of my soul and the souls of people who deserve love, laughter, appreciation, and the freedom to just *be*. Each of us has a liberating purpose, and my hope is that you will receive these lessons and more importantly that you will grow to know that you are worth fighting for and that you are worthy of your freedom.

INTRODUCTION

WHAT'S IN FRONT OF US IS MORE IMPORTANT THAN WHAT'S BEHIND US.

On June 22, 2023, just a day after my fifty-first birthday and thirteen years since my release from prison, my brother Alan and I were invited to the Porsche Driving Experience in Carson, California. We arrived at a large modern facility fronted by a vibrant assortment of Porsches, both new and impeccably preserved vintage models reminiscent of the scaled-down race cars we had played with as kids. If there was a paradise for gearheads, grease monkeys, and car enthusiasts, this was unquestionably it.

By a stroke of luck, my instructor happened to be a fellow Michigan native, and his welcoming charm reminded me of home. We quickly caught up on all things Detroit and Michigan before stepping outside to check out the two cars I would be driving. The first was a sleek yellow 911 GT3, a beautiful beast that blended track-focused capabilities with street-legal practicality. The second was a beautiful burgundy 911 Turbo that did zero to sixty in 2.7 seconds and had no problem pinning my body to the seat.

I hopped into the passenger seat of the yellow 911, and we set off onto the track. We practiced oversteering exercises, going over techniques to recover from a spin. The key was keeping your eyes on where you wanted to go rather than what you were afraid of hitting. Then we switched seats, and it was my turn to navigate the short water-slicked track. After a few spinouts, I finally mastered the maneuver, and I was allowed to launch the Porsche as fast as I could. But the real point of the exercise was still ahead of us.

We headed over to the main track. Covering the rearview mirror, the instructor told me, "I own this mirror, and you have to trust me." Sensing my hesitation, he went on to explain his experience as a professional and stunt driver for over fifteen years. He had encountered every possible scenario on the track and witnessed the consequences of drivers fixating on what was behind them rather than focusing on their intended path. He emphasized that my sole objective on the track should be to concentrate on where I wanted to go. As I took off, a small voice said to me, "Your past doesn't define your path!"

If I genuinely desired to push my heart to the edge by driving this car to its limit, I had to trust my instructor, knowing he had already done all the groundwork.

That is what I'm asking of you: to trust me, knowing that I, too, have already done the groundwork.

I have overcome trauma, grief, guilt, and physical incarceration. I have succeeded beyond anyone's expectations of what was possible for me. I have beat the odds, overcome heartbreak, and developed a deep and profound understanding of the power of forgiveness, both of myself and of others. My hope as we embark together on this journey toward personal freedom is that you will allow me to take the mirror while you take the steering wheel.

How to Use This Book

This book is designed to be both a guide and a companion on your journey to freedom. To get the most from these pages, here's how the different elements work together:

The Three-Part Journey

This book follows a natural progression of liberation:

Part 1: Breaking the Chains
First, we dismantle what holds us back—grief, anger, and shame—examining how these forces create invisible prisons in our lives.

Part 2: Finding Your Strength
Next, we develop strengths that sustain freedom—vulnerability, resilience, and forgiveness—creating a solid foundation for growth.

Part 3: Embracing Freedom
Finally, we construct a life defined by choice rather than circumstance, embracing purpose, joy, success, and lasting freedom.

Elements for Deeper Engagement

Digging Deeper sections invite you to explore beneath the surface of concepts, pushing beyond intellectual understanding to emotional insight. These reflections challenge you to confront difficult truths about yourself and your experiences.

Keys provide practical, actionable steps to implement what you've learned. Consider these your tools for unlocking specific doors on your journey to freedom. They transform abstract concepts into concrete practices you can begin today.

Quotes and nuggets of wisdom appear throughout the text as moments of inspiration and reflection. These distilled wisdom points serve as touchstones, offering clarity during challenging moments and inviting you to pause and consider how these truths apply to your own life.

How to Approach This Work

This isn't a book to rush through. Each chapter builds on the last, but freedom isn't linear—you may find yourself returning to earlier sections as new insights emerge.

I encourage you to

- read with intention, perhaps keeping a journal nearby to record thoughts and insights;
- practice the exercises, even (and especially) the ones that make you uncomfortable;

HOW TO USE THIS BOOK

- be patient with yourself, understanding that transformation takes time; and
- find community where possible, as discussing these concepts with others can deepen your understanding.

Remember, this book doesn't just describe freedom—it's designed to help you experience it. The knowledge here becomes powerful only when applied to your life. Your freedom journey is uniquely yours, but you're not walking it alone.

PART 1

BREAKING THE CHAINS

CHAPTER ONE
GRIEF

I don't want to write this down
I wanna tell you how I feel right now

—Mos Def, "UMI Says"

I stared at the tip of the pen as it pressed into the paper. It was the morning of January 1, 2021. My goal was simple: set my intentions for the year. It was a practice I had adopted while sitting in a prison cell two decades prior.

Writing down the things I desired to manifest in my life had become a consistent practice. However, that day, instead of writing about the future, I was ruminating on the previous year. So many things had changed. My son Sekou and I had moved into our new home, just five months before the US shut down due to COVID. While navigating homeschooling and remote work, we got a pandemic puppy we named Indyego, and I met an amazing woman named Liz.

That spring of 2021, as the moldy gray clouds of winter started to lift, I flew my dad and stepmom out from Detroit to visit me in LA. It was our first time seeing one another in person since the beginning of the pandemic and their first time ever visiting the city. It was heaven. We had lengthy conversations and cocktails by the backyard firepit, my dad and I swam in our pool, we visited the Santa Monica Pier, and we enjoyed meals together. We went to the California African American Museum, where I was honored to be part of an exhibit called "Men of Courage," alongside figures like LeBron James, Ryan Coogler, and Kendrick Lamar. I told them about my new love interest and that I was excited to finally meet her in person.

"Son, a big part of being in a relationship is learning how to receive your significant other's unique way of loving you. If you communicate the way you desire to be loved and are open to them loving you in their way, you will be OK, for the most part," my dad said. He often ended his philosophical musings with "for the most part." I took it to mean that things in a relationship won't always be 100 percent positive but that we will be OK as long as we accept this reality.

The following month, Liz and I were about to meet in person and travel together for the first time. We had been introduced by our mutual friend Trabian in December 2020 through a call that we would later learn we were both reluctant to join. Our conversation flowed effortlessly, and we started talking nightly until we decided to meet in person. Liz flew to LA, and the following day, we flew up north to Half Moon Bay, where we spent a few days hanging out, laughing, eating saltwater taffy, and getting to know each other. We continued our daily calls after Liz headed back to Chicago, and then she returned to help me celebrate my birthday and my homecoming anniversary in June.

I was excited to introduce Liz to more of my friends and nervous about sharing my art with her. I got to do both when my friends Ben and Felicia hosted a reading of my new book. Despite my nerves, I was happy she was able to see me doing what I loved and proud she was there for a standing ovation. We had an incredible time, and I was on top of the world. My work was going well, Sekou was thriving in life and school, my art was evolving, and my heart had been opened to love again.

I was on top of the world.

Then, on July 12, I received a call from my father about my brother. "Sherrod was found shot to death in the kitchen of a house on the west side," he said, his voice cracking. Everything seemed to freeze in that moment—even the music playing in the background. The air was snatched from my lungs, and I couldn't bring myself to utter a word. My fingers and the phone felt like ice blocks. "Sherrod is dead," he managed to get out as his voice descended into a wail that sent chills through my body.

The last time I'd seen Sherrod, we'd stood talking outside of Detroit's Masonic Temple, a magnificent and elegant building that stretched across Third Street like a perfectly executed grand jeté. The frigid November wind whipped around us as we did our best to catch up on everything that had transpired since we'd last seen each other. We talked often by phone, but my life in LA had gotten pretty busy, making it harder to get back to Detroit as often as I wanted to. He had been in prison as well, and his parole made it impossible for him to come and see me in LA.

Sherrod was my stepbrother. We'd met in 1985 when our parents first started dating. He was the youngest of three, and I was the fourth of six. When five years later our parents married, I went from having five siblings to having eight. I was excited to have them: my older stepbrother, Kidd; my older stepsister, Vanessa; and my new little brother, Sherrod, joined my brothers Alan and Art and my sisters Tamica, Nakia, and Shamica. Vanessa and I had the classic teenage tension, but we quickly grew to be best friends. We fought over the phone and made up over the music, fast food, and weed we hid from our parents. Kidd and I connected over sports, and even though we didn't talk a lot growing up, we developed a bond and mutual respect through letters when I went to prison.

With Sherrod it was different from the beginning. When our parents first got together, he was a chubby, shy elementary school kid, and I was excited to finally have a baby brother. I couldn't wait to teach him how to fight the neighborhood bullies, hold his own on the basketball court, and talk to girls. But there was a big problem: Sherrod wasn't interested in any of the things I was interested in. Instead, he wanted to eat snacks and play video games. He became the typical annoying little brother.

Sherrod was a preteen by the time our parents married, and I was sentenced to prison shortly thereafter. I was heartbroken to leave him and the rest of my siblings behind.

About six years into my sentence, he wrote that he was thinking of me because he was wearing a coat I had sent home from prison. His letter touched me profoundly, showing me the void I had left in my family's life.

When I was finally released, I was excited to reconnect with Sherrod and my other siblings, but shortly after I got home, Sherrod was sentenced to eight years in prison for shooting three people. They were from our neighborhood—they'd grown up just down the street. Word on the street was they had attacked Sherrod and his girlfriend, beating them both when he refused to give them money. He got a gun, went back down the street, and shot *and injured* all three of them.

I went to his sentencing and couldn't help thinking that I somehow had failed to keep him out of the system. Over the years I had sent letters home urging the young men in my family and neighborhood not to make the same poor decisions I had. "Don't let a thirty-second decision become a life sentence," I would often write, repeating what I had heard in the prison yard over the years.

Now here I was imagining Sherrod going through the hell I had just broken free from. The thought of the strip searches, the violence, and the indignity of it all was heartbreaking. I tried to keep my composure, and I promised Sherrod I would be there for him and make sure he made the best of his time. My hard time inside had earned me friends and relationships at the same prison where he now was. I knew I could rely on them to keep my brother safe and on the right track.

Throughout his incarceration, I sent him books that had inspired me, such as *As a Man Thinketh* by James Allen, *Think and Grow Rich* by Napoleon Hill, *The Secret* by Rhonda Byrne, and books about artists, entrepreneurs, and historic figures. I also made sure he had great mentors and encouraged him to take advantage of whatever classes were being offered. He wrote me often, and I was impressed with his intellectual growth and perspective. Through our letters and phone calls, he shared things we'd never been able to discuss before: his parents' divorce, our parents' marriage, and all the feelings those experiences evoked. Our parents never talked to us about any of these things—they just threw us all together and hoped for the best. Our parents' generation gave birth to the words "Fuck them kids," something we joke and laugh about today. So we found and fought our way from being stepsiblings to full-on siblings. Eventually, there was no distinction—we were simply family.

I promised Sherrod that I would come to see him, but it was years before my visit was approved by the prison administration, despite us being family. One day Sherrod called to tell me he was taking a class and the textbook they were using had included some excerpts of writings I had done while in prison. His excitement and pride were palpable, and I told him that it meant the world to me that my words were being used to help imprisoned men find their own voices. I also told him about the challenges of buying a house, hustling books, and making my way legally. We even laughed about my experiences with some of the foods I had discovered since being home, like sushi, octopus, and wagyu. Anytime he saw me on TV or read about me in a publication he had access to, he would find a way to get in touch simply to let me know it made him more determined to do the right thing when he came home.

I was so excited for his homecoming. I wanted to share my adventures with him. I wanted him to see the Pacific Ocean and be blown away the way I had been the first time I saw it. I wanted him to travel abroad, eat weird foods, and find his own sense of peace and purpose the way I had found mine. We even talked about him joining me out in LA once he got off parole.

True to his word, Sherrod stayed focused on his education. He earned his associate's degree in prison and was working on his master's degree, which he completed shortly after he was released. It was a big moment for our family, and I was so proud of him because I knew how hard it is to stay committed to a goal and harder still when you have a felony on your record.

My baby brother was defying the odds and dreaming of new possibilities when his life was abruptly ended by gunfire, making him another in a long line of casualties in an environment where escaping the odds seems as impossible as getting a master's degree.

Like many people getting out of prison, Sherrod was trying to figure his life out. Now he was dead, and the details of his murder were infuriating. The suspected killer was someone my brother thought of as a friend. He had broken bread at our family's dining room table and acted the part of a good friend. I was devastated, heartbroken, and compressed in a furious swirl of feelings: anger, sadness, thoughts of revenge, shame, and guilt. I had devastated a family, and now my family was devastated. I had taken a life and inflicted the same pain my family was now feeling. I dried my tears and stuffed my feelings down, but they were raging.

I called Liz, tears streaming down my face. Without hesitation, she offered to fly out and help me pack my suitcase for the long trip home. I said no, but in her wisdom, she came anyway. Once she got to LA, I asked her to come with me to Detroit, and she did. Her presence and ability to navigate all the logistics allowed me to be fully present for my parents and siblings. The weight of grief isn't meant to be carried alone, and despite being in the midst of an emotional storm, I could see clearly that Liz was here to stay. Our angels show up when we need them most.

On the plane, I pulled up my laptop and used the time to liberate the words that were choking me, caught somewhere between the pit of my stomach and the back of my throat. I had never imagined I'd have to navigate trying to grieve while knowing I, too, had killed a man. I knew that if I did not write, I would unravel. I dumped the contents of my heart and mind into a letter, the first draft of which was like raw sewage. But I kept refining and finished it in the parking lot of the hotel:

> I am writing to the person who took Sherrod's life. Though you don't know me personally, you know my family. You know the details of our family home, the sound of my parents' laughter, the taste of food cooked and served with the same love that the rest of our family friends have come to enjoy. So although you didn't know me personally, our lives are connected in a way that I wish was not possible that extends from my little brother's life to his death. Thirty years ago, in July 1991, I made a terrible and regrettable decision. I shot and

killed a man. He was not just a man—he was a father, son, husband, and beloved friend to those who knew him. This past weekend, you also shot and killed a man—my younger brother, Sherrod. He was a son, uncle, brother, and friend to many. Although I only have fragments of the circumstances that led to my brother's death, the reality is that we both have caused immeasurable pain and grief for the families of the men we took from this world.

My brother's life was more than a collection of moments; it was a complex tapestry of what it means to be human, incomplete and imperfect in all the ways a life lived exists. Despite my brother's struggles and his past, he was on the right path, and his life was valuable. I pause here because I wonder, in your reckless disregard for Sherrod's life, did you hold the belief that life is only valuable when it fits into a neat, tidy box or when it is free from the struggles and challenges of everyday life? As I reflect on my brother's death, I feel a range of emotions, including anger and heartbreak. It is a harsh reality that weighs heavily on my soul, and I feel a tremendous amount of guilt knowing that I have caused another family to experience the same pain and loss that my own family is going through. It is a terrible burden to bear to be both a victim and a perpetrator of gun violence.

Nothing can bring my brother back, just as nothing can bring the man I killed back to life. That is a reality that weighs heavily on my soul as I now imagine what it is going to be like to wander through Detroit, seeing empty faces everywhere

I look. Nothing will ever be the same again. Our family will never again hear my brother's laughter or listen to his endless jokes and dreams for the future. Our friends on Ferguson Street where Sherrod and I grew up will never be able to drive or walk past our home where they were welcomed and look at it the same way.

The joy and excitement that once characterized my parents' home have been replaced by grief and profound anger. The pride I once had for Detroit has been shattered in a way I never could have imagined. As I now sit in the parking lot of my hotel, all I can think about is every other place I would rather be right now, like back home in LA. But here I am, just days away from laying my brother to rest, knowing that my soul will never be the same again.

Even amid horrendous loss, my thoughts were about your soul, and it was a contradiction to other base-level thinking. On one hand, I was angry, and on the other hand, I was finding my way to compassion. I thought about how terrible your own trauma must have been to lead you down this path. I was confused, and still, my hope was that one day, you would find the healing and the peace I believe humans are capable of. I hoped that you would find the strength to confront your own demons and make amends for the pain you have caused. And most of all, I hoped that you would find a way to contribute something positive and meaningful to the world as a way of honoring Sherrod's life and the lives that have been forever changed by your actions.

I wondered if you felt the same, if you were wracked with the guilt of killing Sherrod and the grief of knowing your friend is now dead. I wondered if you regretted the callous decision to leave my brother's body to be discovered by his father and big sister. I wondered if you understood the weight of what you had done, the ripple effect that your actions have had on our families and our neighborhood. I wondered if you were capable of empathy and remorse or if you were consumed by anger and violence.

But most of all, I wondered why. Why did you choose to pull the trigger, to end my brother's life and shatter so many others? What could have been going through your mind in that moment, what could have justified taking another human being's life? I don't know if these questions will ever be answered or if the pain of my brother's loss will lessen over time. But I hope you find a way to understand the gravity of what you have done and the impact it has had on so many people. I hope you find a way to make amends and seek forgiveness before your death, not just for yourself, but for all of those who have been affected by your actions.

Sincerely,
Shaka

> I ain't no perfect man
> I'm trying to do, the best that I can
> With what it is I have

> I ain't no perfect man
> I'm trying to do, the best that I can
> With what it is I have

When I returned to LA after laying Sherrod to rest, I descended into a deep state of grieving, a labyrinth of sadness, anger, and guilt. Questions about my own mortality, the future of my son and all the boys who came from where I came from, swarmed into my consciousness like hornets defending their nest. What could I have done differently? Why does violent death happen so often to those who come from where I come from? Is God angry with me? What if we had grown up in another environment? What if Sherrod had been paroled to LA to live with me and start his life over out here?

Like many who find themselves in grief, I was self-flagellating. I beat my ass with question after question, each one whipping down on me, barely giving me time to recover. My thoughts were stuck like cars slogging through LA traffic. It was one of the toughest parts of grieving: one moment you're laughing or enjoying a moment, and boom, like a sledgehammer crashing through drywall, a hole is knocked into you.

Patching, spackling, and smoothing that hole over took time, presence, and action. The first step was accepting grief along with the anger and shame that it opened inside of me. "My little brother is dead": Just saying it out loud allowed me to start moving my mind and heart forward. Slowly but surely, I allowed myself to mourn Sherrod and all the new things I wouldn't get a chance to share with him and that he would never achieve or experience. I thought about him never getting the chance to be a dad, a husband, or a homeowner.

Some years ago, I heard someone on TV say the most important part of our lives is the dash between the day we are born and the day we die. March 11, 1978—dash—July 9, 2021. That was my brother's dash. What did it mean? It meant my brother had lived a life full of laughter, love, and loss and that we were lucky to have him here with us for that time. That's what I clung to, to get back to living my life. The dash of grief between when Sherrod was born and died had given me a new way of seeing things. Grief came bearing the gift of presence, which forced me to zero in on gratitude. Despite the heartbreak of his death, I had a deep sense of gratitude for his existence. Reflecting on his absence made me more thankful for the time we got to share while he was here in the physical. My gratitude was so strong that it recentered me with an understanding that being thankful is one of the greatest ways to experience the magic of this thing called life.

After the funeral repast was over, all the condolence letters read and acknowledged, and my two weeks of bereavement leave over, I told myself to jump back into the swing of life. In reality my journey of grieving my brother was just getting underway.

I was now existing in a state of high-functioning grief. I went back to work, took countless Zoom meetings and phone calls, trained some teams, and helped close some deals. On and on it went. Grief goes everywhere and nowhere. It hides between the cracks of moments, sometimes as a robber and sometimes as a gift bearer. Grief doesn't have a pause button; it doesn't wait. Sometimes it leaps at you; other times it crawls upon you, subtly nuzzling up to you, as you find yourself in a ball of tears, or in a burst of anger, or in a knot of depression. At other times it has you smiling and laughing at a memory of your loved one. There's an ugly magic to it, the way that it manifests in these moments.

When I became empty from grief, I filled myself up with work projects and home projects. Instead, I should have said "Fuck it all" and taken the time out to really heal myself. Allowing ourselves to grieve fully and honestly is an act of liberation. It's a master key capable of unlocking all the other prison doors we find ourselves behind. No one gets through life without loss or grief, but you can free yourself from the anger, guilt, and depression it brings.

Beginning to break free from the grip of grief, I couldn't entirely control the waves of emotion, but I could allow myself to stop and acknowledge those emotions in their entirety. I learned to show myself grace, tenderness, and thoughtfulness. Grace means allowing yourself to lean into your feelings to fully process them. Tenderness means giving yourself permission to grieve and leaning into your support system. Thoughtfulness means extending that grace to others and communicating effectively with those around you.

I also learned that grief can manifest in various counterproductive ways: in unfolded laundry, dishes piling up in the sink, lashing out at loved ones, oversleeping, undersleeping, overeating, drinking in excess, and smoking more. I was grumpy, impatient, less kind, and more focused on goals instead of the people in my life.

The heavy parts were the guilt, the anger, and the survivor's remorse. Over and over, I interrogated myself like a suspect on *The First 48*. What could I have done? What could I have said? What steps could I have taken to help change the outcomes?

Yes, I was healing, but I was having a reckoning simultaneously. There was the grief of losing my brother and the guilt of my own misdeeds. It was knocking me silly.

In the past whenever I was hurting, I would turn that hurt into energy to succeed or accomplish some external goal. But in the process, I was imprisoning myself by directing that creative energy outward instead of inward.

To free myself from this prison of grief, I prayed deeply; meditated daily; created a gratitude mantra that included something I had read many years ago that said *I am thankful, even for this*; and wrote out my thoughts about life. With each word written or spoken, I found myself climbing out, moment by moment, while thinking about how proud and amazed my Sherrod would be. Nearly three years after Sherrod's death, I came across this passage while reading *Tuesdays with Morrie* by Mitch Albom. While talking to Mitch about a dream, Morrie said, "'That's what we're all looking for. A certain peace with the idea of dying. If we know, in the end, that we can ultimately have that peace with dying, then we can finally do the really hard thing.' Which is? 'Make peace with living.'"

Not all of us get to prepare for or make peace with death. Sherrod certainly didn't. But as long as we are breathing, we can be present in life while making peace with grief. With that knowledge I shifted my focus to what I could do with those around me. I could share my love, lessons, and resources and be fully present with the people in my life. But it had to start with me.

One night, three months after Sherrod was buried, the LA autumn was slogging by in a haze of blazing-hot days and beautifully warm nights. Liz and I were at home winding down after packing for an upcoming trip. Earlier in the day, we'd dropped our dog, Indy, off with a new trainer, and the house felt quiet without him. Just before settling into the evening, my phone rang. It was the trainer calling to meet him at the veterinary clinic. Indy had been hit by a car and killed. I couldn't believe this shit.

    I rushed to the vet. The vet took me to the back to see my boy. He looked serene, like he was peacefully sleeping under a cover. But he wasn't sleeping—our big, beautiful boy was now dead. I held back my anger with Herculean effort as I slumped back to my SUV. I sat for what felt like hours trying to gather myself, though I'm sure it was only minutes. The vision of Indy lying dead in a cold vet hospital collided with the image I had of Sekou being home tucked safely in the warmth of his bed and the vision of Liz waiting for me to walk in the door.

    I played back the conversation with the trainer in my head. He said Indy had slipped out of his collar after trying to bite a pedestrian. The knot in my stomach clenched tighter, as I sensed he was lying. I wanted to jump out of the truck and confront him. I was in a dark place and spiraling. The darkest, repressed part of me was urging me to seek revenge, not just for Indy, but for Sherrod. As Carl Jung said, "Unfortunately there can be no doubt that man is, on the whole, less good than he imagines himself or wants to be. Everyone carries a shadow, and the less it is embodied in the individual's conscious life, the blacker and denser it is."

When Sherrod was murdered, some members of our family and the homies on the block wanted blood and retaliation, but I talked them down. It was counterintuitive to my anger and the code of the street I had been raised in, but I was exhausted from seeing our community caught in the loop of trauma and violence. My core philosophy that "everyone is redeemable" was now being challenged internally. I was proud of how I led the homies and our family through it while repressing my own thoughts of revenge.

But here I was again fighting my shadow. Then it hit me: it was too late to protect Sherrod or Indy. They were both gone. The only ones I could now protect were at home, one sleeping and the other waiting for me to return. I had to go home. I sped out of the parking lot, holding back a river of tears that were threatening to break through the dam.

The next morning, I lay in bed, aimlessly scrolling through Instagram, when I jumped to the trainer's page and saw him with his daughter playing with a beautiful German shepherd. The video sent me spiraling back into a smoldering rage. I wanted to run his dog over so he could feel how we felt. The shadow had been reawakened.

I knew I would never act on those thoughts, but I needed to feel the raw emotion of my anger, and I needed to confront those destructive ideas. After all, one can't truly know if they have changed unless they are faced with something that challenges their sense of who they are. So here I was confronting my shadow, trying to grieve and love simultaneously. I shared my dark fantasy with Liz, who helped me purge my heart and truly grieve. The death of Indy, coming so soon after Sherrod's murder, unearthed emotions that I thought I'd processed.

I had to finally accept that my brother Sherrod wasn't coming back, that Indy wasn't coming back, and that our lives would be forever changed. But beneath the grief, there was anger—a raw, burning rage at the unfairness of it all. And then there was shame, creeping in like an unwelcome guest. Shame for what I didn't see, for what I couldn't change, and for the questions that wouldn't stop haunting me: Should I have done more? Could I have prevented this? Could I have vetted the trainer more thoroughly or read more Yelp reviews? The grief, the anger, the shame—they were all tangled together. This realization was pivotal; it showed me that healing is not only about coping with loss but also about confronting and understanding the complex layers of emotions that accompany it.

Coming out on the other side doesn't mean that you forget. I could never forget about my brother Sherrod or our beautiful puppy Indy. In fact, the opposite is true; grieving allowed me to be thankful and remember the beautiful and sacred moments even more. In the early stages after Sherrod's and Indy's deaths,

I was numb, then angry, then sad. I was angry at my city, at my hood, at the man who shot my brother, at the trainer, and at life. Coming out on the other side gave me a deeper commitment to ending gun violence, loving shamelessly, and preparing myself to love the next puppy that comes into my life.

Nearly three years after Sherrod's and Indy's deaths, I was tentatively feeling like things were looking up. I left the company where I had been working and ventured back out on my own as an entrepreneur. Liz and I had grown deeply in love, gotten engaged, and were preparing for our wedding. Sekou was thriving in school, getting all A's; playing football, basketball, and soccer; and making new friends. He had been a stellar student at Baldwin Elementary and had teachers who adored him there. In his new middle school, he was playing piano, enjoying video games, and just being a kid. He was excelling at everything with an ease that blew my mind.

Then one day Sekou was rushed to the ER, where a scary few hours led to a three-day hospitalization and a diagnosis of type 1 diabetes. A new chamber of grief had now been opened in my heart. I was now grieving the loss of Sekou's seeming invulnerability and the comfort of being his protector. "Am I going to die, Dad?" Sekou asked me as we sat outside in the hospital courtyard. "No, son, you aren't going to die," I said with all the confidence I could muster while internally falling apart. I knew I wasn't the only parent facing this question, as I had seen many teary parents walking the halls of the pediatric unit.

This was my baby boy, the wunderkind who showed up in love and curiosity and with the most charming smile. My intelligent little artist, whom I'd managed to shield from the evils I had seen as a kid. But now his own body was turning on him.

After assuring him that he wasn't going to die, I said, "Son, sometimes the universe gives its warriors battles they didn't ask for, but when a warrior embraces those unwelcome battles, they become a gift to themselves and others. You are a warrior, your name, Sekou Akili, means scholarly leader, and if there is anyone who can lead through a difficult time, it is you, son. Together we will win this battle, but you must lead us, because this battle was given to you!"

"I will lead it, Dad," he responded as he leaned on my shoulder. With one hand, I combed my fingers through his hair while wiping the tears from my eyes with the other.

Grief's Unforgiving Nature

As the saying goes, hindsight is twenty-twenty. But grief distorts our perception. I've spent countless hours asking myself the tough questions: Did I miss signals about Sekou's health? Could I have found a better trainer for Indy? How could I have prevented Sherrod's incarceration or murder? This kind of self-interrogation can become a heavy blanket of shame, leading to a life filled with regret, anger, and doubt.

There are so many forms of grief in this life—grieving past decisions, lost friendships, ended relationships, loss of youth, and jobs we've left behind. Each comes with its own set of regrets and questions: Did I quit too soon? Did I give enough? Did I do enough research? Did I give my all? Grieving these losses can be just as profound and lingering as the grief of a lost loved one.

The Weight of Anger and Healing

Grief often brings anger, an emotion that can feel as relentless as dandelions on a hillside. For me, anger blossomed uncontrollably, and there was no blowing away the pollen or making a wish. I had to sit with it, confront it, and let it be. Like an inexperienced swimmer fighting a riptide, I kept struggling against the current of my own emotions, hoping that somewhere out there, a lifeguard would come to save me from myself.

In those dark moments, I would sit up and talk to Liz, who would take my hand and listen as I vented about the unfairness of it all. I wanted to act on my anger, to unleash it, but I knew that wasn't who I wanted to be anymore. It's a mindfuck to try to grieve and love simultaneously, especially when our culture doesn't create space for us to feel fully human.

Finding Resilience and Purpose

Grief has taught me the importance of finding purpose and sticking to it, of not letting anything get in the way. It made me appreciate the moments, experiences, people, and pets even more. Over time, I found solace in Mos Def's song "UMI Says," which became my morning anthem—a reminder to keep going, to honor my pain, and to use it as fuel.

Grief comes in layers, each one peeling back to reveal another layer of pain or memory. I miss the arguments my brother and I had, the inside jokes, the barbecues on Ferguson Street, and the days when our house was full of music, laughter, and life. None of my friends died peaceful deaths; they were victims of carnage, flesh, and twisted metal, a not-uncommon outcome in our neighborhood. This is a reality I hoped I'd escaped—but pain and loss are part of life. And now I miss Indy and our walks through our peaceful neighborhood, and I miss the spontaneity of grabbing ice cream or a slice of pizza with Sekou without counting carbs or him having to jab himself with a needle.

Finding Light amid Darkness

Grief is a master teacher, and in its lessons, we find the strength to keep moving forward. Sherrod's death imprinted a new picture of our family dynamics, one that we are still learning to navigate. Our absent loved ones are the missing pieces that complete our picture, reminding us that no one deserves to be left alone in a vacant house of memories.

Grief may never fully release its grip, but it shapes us, molds us, and in its own painful way, propels us to find meaning in the moments we have left. It teaches us that the journey is not about overcoming grief but about carrying it with us, allowing it to be a part of our story without letting it define us.

DIGGING DEEPER

Here's what I want you to do in this moment. I want you to stop and do a reflection meditation. How is grief showing up in your life? What are all the different ways it has shown up?

Thinking about my answers to this question and writing them down is what helped me unearth the myths I'd been telling myself. Seeing the myths was the first step in breaking free of them and in learning to communicate effectively with those who were truly there to help me.

> Myth 1: You have a limited amount of time to get over grief.
> Myth 2: Grief comes to an end at some point.
> Myth 3: You will never experience joy, love, or success again.
> Myth 4: It won't get better.

These myths, like so many falsehoods we tell ourselves, create hidden bars that are hard to see and even harder to escape. The reality, however, is that grief has no strict timeline, allowing each person to navigate their loss uniquely and authentically. While grief may feel like it will never end, it can evolve and become a less overwhelming part of life that we learn to carry differently over time. Contrary to the myth that grief precludes future joy, love, or success, these experiences can indeed coexist with grief, often reminding us to embrace a spirit of gratitude for the time we have left with those we love. Finally, although it may seem initially impossible, grief does become more manageable, gradually transforming into a source of resilience, deeper understanding, and renewed purpose.

KEYS TO PROCESSING GRIEF

1. Create Space for Grief
- Set aside dedicated time to feel your emotions fully. This might be during a quiet hour alone or a visit to a meaningful place.
- Allow yourself to cry, write, or simply sit with your feelings without judgment.

2. Honor Grief's Nonlinear Nature
- Understand that grief doesn't follow a predictable timeline.
- Accept fluctuations as normal rather than signs of regression or weakness.

3. Practice Grace, Tenderness, and Thoughtfulness
- Show yourself grace by leaning into your feelings to fully process them.
- Practice tenderness by giving yourself permission to grieve and relying on your support system.
- Extend thoughtfulness to others by communicating your needs effectively.

4. Practice Connection, Not Isolation
- Share your experience with others who can sit with you in your pain without trying to rush to your healing.
- Remember that grief carried alone becomes heavier.

Remember that allowing yourself to grieve fully and honestly is an act of liberation. It's a master key capable of unlocking all the other prison doors we find ourselves behind.

No one gets through life without loss, but you can free yourself from the anger, guilt, and depression it brings by embracing the process rather than fighting against it.

CHAPTER TWO
ANGER

You will not be punished for your anger, you will be punished by your anger.

—Buddha

My anger was an uninvited guest, akin to a phantom who infiltrates someone's home and takes up residence without the owner's knowledge. As a child, I never saw myself as angry—quite the opposite. I was the well-behaved, easy-to-get-along-with, promising young kid who earned scholarships and made the honor roll. I won praise from my friends' parents for being kind and courteous and was the kid my family saw as a beacon of hope for a successful future. My parents enthusiastically encouraged me to read to my grandparents and showed off my artwork when they visited, and my uncle John dragged me out of bed to dance like Michael Jackson for the family. I was a cool and handsome kid with lofty dreams, and I envisioned myself becoming an artist or doctor—occupations I believed were both noble and creatively altruistic. In that childhood dream, I could serve people or create in a way that helped people feel better.

All that changed when my trust was betrayed in the worst way imaginable. I went from the kid who shoveled the neighbor's snow and picked fruit from their trees for them to the kid stealing from the store and getting into dustups at school. That bright, young scholarly boy with so much promise was now donning a mask of toughness and acting out in ways that were outside the margins of how he was raised. Though I didn't have the right language for it back then, I was a wounded child who grew into a violent young man, causing harm to many, including myself.

As I got older, I increasingly lost control of my emotions, getting angrier and more daring in my juvenile exploits. I thought my anger was a source of power. But in truth, my anger had trapped me, locking me in an internal cage that ultimately led to physical imprisonment and solitary confinement.

Several years into my sentence, I experienced a particularly dark time. In solitary and unable to retaliate against the man in the next cell, I was left with nothing but my rage-filled thoughts and nowhere for them to go. I picked up a pen and began to write with brutal honesty, pouring out everything I'd been holding inside. What became painfully clear as the words filled the page was that my anger wasn't just controlling me—it was suffocating what little good I had left inside me.

I discovered the author Louis L'Amour while I was in solitary confinement. His words came back to me: "Anger is a killing thing: it kills the man who angers, for each rage leaves him less than he had been before—it takes something from him." Anger had stripped me of everything, including my freedom. It stripped me of self-control, dignity, and the ability to peacefully coexist with others. But in that solitary cell, reading through my own words in a moment of stillness, I resolved to take back everything the anger had stolen: my sense of emotional safety, self-love, and purpose. All were mine to reclaim.

The Rage Cage

The jangling keys, the scraping open of metal footlockers, and the occasional profanity-laced outburst formed a discordant symphony—the soundtrack of solitary confinement at Oaks Correctional Facility in western Michigan. It was February, one of the coldest of months in Michigan, with relentless snowfalls that blanketed the prison yard for days on end.

I waited, as usual, for the changing of the guard—the morning crew relieving the night shift—before reluctantly pulling myself from my bunk. I used the dull steel toilet in the corner of my cell before brushing my teeth in the rusty sink that was attached to it. As I returned to my bunk, I glanced out the tiny window to see workers dressed in dingy kitchen whites, pushing food carts through a foot of snow, backbreaking work that made me ponder the irony of full employment in prison (we started at seventeen cents an hour) and rampant joblessness in the neighborhoods most of us came from.

After inhaling my breakfast of watery green eggs, damp burnt toast, and stony grits, I waited for the officer's morning question: Do you want to go outside for an hour of recreation? The officers hated taking us outside, and I equally despised those cages, eight in a row, no bigger than dog kennels. But even in the arctic cold, going to the yard was the only option for getting out of my cell, even if just for an hour five days a week. The tier had been relatively quiet in the past couple of days, and not many of the men had been going out due to the cold. But I yearned for fresh air, a reprieve from the stench and madness of the cell block. When the officer came by, I nodded, affirming my intention to brave the frigid outdoors—after all, it was only for an hour.

My prison wardrobe basically consisted of a thin faded blue-and-orange state-issued jacket, cheap plastic shoes, and gloves better suited for gardening than the cold. Handcuffed and shackled, I trudged down the tier. The cuffs bit into my ankles with each step, one of the many painful costs of accessing fresh air. I stepped into the stabbing cold. I began to regret leaving the semiwarmth of the cell block, but my lungs and skin craved being outside, so I pushed on. From one of the cages nearby, a man we called Two Toned due to his uneven and bumpy skin made some wisecrack. I acknowledged him but kept my response terse. He had a reputation for talking big within the safety of his cell but showed less bravado on the general population yard. We called men like Two Toned cell gangsters: guys who talked shit when tucked safely behind the cells in solitary confinement but clammed up when confronted on the yard.

I had no desire to associate with him or any of the other shit talkers in solitary. I had learned early on from the old heads: "If a man isn't willing to serve a life sentence or die for you, don't consider him a true friend." It was our distorted way of marking friendship. The prison yard was filled with fleeting allegiances of convenience, and I sought to avoid the drama.

But Two Toned was heading out to the yard, and as officers went about the business of removing our cuffs, he began to talk shit. The officers merely smirked.

Over the next hour, I ran around in a tight circle between sets of push-ups. With my hour drawing to an end, I was damp and freezing, but the officers weren't in a rush to bring us back in. Instead, every few minutes one of the officers would stick his head out of the cellblock door, only to close it with a laugh. They were deliberately stretching out our time in the bitter cold, a crude reminder of the power they held. This was only a glimpse of the brutality inherent within the system, where one person's actions could lead to consequences for everyone. I hated paying the price for other people's fuckups, and Two Toned had fucked up, leaving the rest of us to pay the tab. Hours later, when the officers were hustling me back to my cell, I was battling both the bone-chilling cold and a rising storm of rage. My helplessness in the situation triggered my anger, and I was trying hard to keep my shit together. It was a battle that I felt myself losing.

With my feet and hands numb from the cold, I looked the officers dead in the eye and swore to them that when, not if, I got out of there, I was going to fuck them up. One of them returned my glare and uttered, "You ain't never getting out of here, motherfucker." His acerbic words were piercing, and I felt my frozen fist fighting to clench as the handcuffs tightened around my wrist.

Damn, what if I never get out of here? I had men nearby who had been in solitary for ten and twenty years.

Back in my bunk, I heard a rapid succession of thumps on my cell wall. It was John, a guy in the cell next door, who had just come from the protective custody unit. "Can I get a couple of cigs on credit until the next store run? I promise I will pay everything I owe." John had been owing me money for cigarettes for two weeks prior, and I couldn't believe he had the audacity to ask me for more on credit. John ignited my already short fuse, and I snapped: "Man, fuck you. You ain't paid what you owe yet." A few minutes later, he decided to retaliate by blowing out the power in my cell using a staple from a magazine. It was one of the ways the men in solitary waged war on one another. This power outage meant I couldn't play jazz on the little radio I used to block out the noise and chaos of the environment. The assaults of the day kept coming: first from the officers, then the frigid temperatures, and now this power outage. My anger had reached the tipping point. "Bitch I'm going to kill you when I get a chance, I don't give a fuck if I have to come over to the protection unit to get your ho ass," I threatened beneath the door.

For the next hour or so, I plotted my revenge. My mind raced like the proverbial hamster on a wheel with an endless loop of fantasies of revenge. There was no way for me to get to John or the officers in a way that would satisfy my anger without punishing myself. So instead I was forced to face my anger head-on. Anger had consumed my latter teenage years and my young adulthood, leading to fights, shootouts, robberies, and everything in between. It was a life I was weary of, a life of deep suffering. Unlike the Fyodor Dostoevsky quote from "The Dream of a Ridiculous Man," I didn't want to suffer so that I may love, I wanted to love and be free of anger so that I no longer suffered.

After pacing my cell floor and calming myself down, I sat back on my bunk, lowered my head, and began to meditate and then to pray. I meditated to clear the fogginess of the moment and prayed to free myself, both mentally and physically. But I was also in the deep throes of a pity-and-woe-is-me party when a powerful thought struck me: I needed to express my angry thoughts, to write about the darkness that had engulfed me. It was terrifying.

A voice told me to let it all out, no matter how painful or shameful. I took the flimsy state-issued plastic pen and began to detail what I would do to my neighbor John whenever I got the chance. The more I detailed my fantasies, the more I desired to stop writing, but I forged ahead, hoping to sate the anger I was feeling. I was also being forced to acknowledge the truth of who I had become. In year two of solitary, at twenty-eight years old, serving my ninth year in prison, I faced these haunting questions: How much worse would I become if I didn't change? How did I go from a dream of being a doctor to serving out my most promising years in prison? Why was I quick to anger and violence when things didn't go my way? Journaling about harming John led to a profound process that was both gut wrenching and enlightening. I had been through so much trauma that my authentic, fun-loving, happy self had been completely buried. The more I wrote, the more the details of my traumatic journey allowed me to see that I was solely responsible for what would happen in the rest of my life. Only I could unlock the cage door that held me in bondage. It didn't matter if the officer was right about me never getting out, if John continued to be a pusillanimous asshole, or if I was forced to freeze in exchange for the chance to breathe some fresh air—the rest of my life was all on me. I had a choice in how I felt and more importantly how I acted.

So I wrote. I journaled about the pain, the rage, the betrayals, and my own misdeeds. Journaling isn't a passive set-it-and-forget-it deal; it's not just jotting some shit down. Active journaling forces you to get off your ass and grab your life by the reins. You have to obsess over the details and dig down to where the truth lives. Despite the physical confinement, writing gave me the satisfaction of moving forward. Sitting with my truth forced me toward action.

I wrote as a man desperate to understand himself, hoping to find a path toward transformation. These pages were both a clash of the Titans and an escape from the abyss, a release from my past, my rage, and my confinement. As Thich Nhat Hanh so aptly put it, "Letting go gives us freedom and freedom is the only condition for happiness." It was a journey that began with acknowledging my shame, disappointments, and failures—hoping it would lead me to the most joyful and liberating experiences of my life. It also forced me to confront all the fucked-up things that had happened to me and to reassign responsibility to those who had caused me harm.

Reassigning responsibility was one of the most powerful breakthroughs I discovered through journaling. Yes, I was ultimately responsible for my healing, but I was not responsible for the things that broke me in the first place.

When Broken Trust Turns Anger to Rage

Growing up on Camden Street was like growing up on a block of superheroes. The men and women on our block mostly had jobs that were celebrated and honored on our school's career day. My father was in the Air Force Reserve, and a friend's dad who lived two doors over was in the Marines. Our dads drew the awe of the kids on the block with their neatly pressed uniforms, fit bodies, and patches that signaled their rank. There was a woman neighbor who was a police officer and another who was a nurse. However, there were two men on the block who stood out to us more than the others. One was Walter King, a man who held a black belt in karate and competed in martial arts and won a lot—I mean a whole lot. His living room bore witness to his winning, with trophies that were bigger than me. The other was a man named CM who lived across the street from us, who also claimed to be a black belt. He didn't have any trophies to prove it, but he did a masterful job of convincing us that he was the baddest Black martial artist in Detroit, if not in the world. He even told us that he had trained with famed Black karate-champ-turned-movie-star Jim Kelly.

His bragging about his karate prowess often left me and my friends arguing about who would win if he and Walter King ever got into a fight. Our arguments got intense as we pointed out their strengths and weaknesses. While Walter King was bigger and more muscular, CM was trim and fit, and he told us that he'd trained with the best in the world. For us it all came down to power versus speed. I mean, it was the late '70s and '80s when karate and kung fu were our life. But as intense as our arguments were, they brought us more joy than anger.

During that time martial arts was everything in our neighborhood. We traded Bruce Lee posters and discussed the kung fu films we watched on Saturdays. There was even a karate school around the corner from our house. I remember the older boys wearing karate shoes for fashion and us kids using broomsticks, chain links, and rusty nails to make nunchucks. So those beloved martial arts heroes towered over the other hardworking men and women on our block.

It was a Saturday evening when my friends and I all decided to go to the double feature that CM held about once a month at his house. He charged fifty cents or so for each kid, provided popcorn, and sold penny candy. As we stood outside CM's house along with his nieces and nephews eating candy while awaiting entry, we wondered aloud if he was going to show us *Enter the Dragon* or scare the life out of us with the Michael Myers character in *Halloween*. Either way, we were prepared to be scared or fired up to practice karate moves on one another. We watched the movies and ate candy and popcorn until late in the evening. When it was time for us to go, CM asked if any of us wanted to spend the night and watch more movies with his nephew and nieces, since they were going to be staying over. They were excited to have us for a slumber party, and we were excited by the promise of more snacks. I ran across the street and pleaded with my mother to let me stay, and when she agreed, I ran back across the street excitedly.

We spent the next couple of hours watching movies and playing in the basement. When it was time for us all to go to bed, CM started assigning sleeping areas to each of us. Two kids could take his son's bed, a couple could sleep on the couch, and his son and I could sleep in his bedroom on the floor. Back in the day, it wasn't uncommon to make what we called pallets on the floor of a family member's or friend's house when we slept over, so I thought nothing of it. We went into his bedroom and lay on top of the blankets we had piled up on the floor and drifted off to sleep. I don't know how long I was in a slumber when I felt a hand on my shoulder nudging me awake. It was CM, and he was whispering. The early part of what he whispered is a bit fuzzy, but what I remember most is him asking me if I wanted to play with him. I was confused about why he wanted to play late at night and said as much. He then asked if I wanted to get in his bed naked and play with him. My heart began pounding in my chest. My parents had warned us of bad men and women who wanted to do weird stuff with kids, though they never quite said what weird stuff was. But what CM was asking sounded like weird stuff. I started to get scared and felt like I was somehow going to get in trouble with my parents, but I still wanted to go home. I would rather face them than be in that room with that weird man asking me weird questions. I told CM I wanted to go home. Gripping my shoulders tightly, he said I couldn't go home tonight but could go and lie on the couch with the other kids. He also gritted his teeth and told me not to say a word to my parents.

I rushed out of his room and into the living room and stuffed myself as deep into a corner of the couch as I could. In that moment I hated CM and everything I had once loved about him. I hated the smell of his house, the cheap popcorn, and the grandiose stories of being a martial artist. I swore to myself that I was going to learn karate and kick his ass when I was older and strong enough. I knew I was too small to fight him and was lucky that I was precocious enough to know that something wasn't right. I remember lying on the couch afraid to go to sleep while wondering about the other kids in the neighborhood. I remembered that some kids stopped coming around or attending the Saturday movies, even some of his own nieces and nephews. But no one ever said why. It all started to make sense.

When I got home the next morning, I wanted to tell my father and mother, but I was too ashamed and afraid. Like many parents of that era, my parents hadn't created the space for us to feel confident coming to them.

I said nothing. The fear lingered, but I could also feel it turning into anger and resolve. I had to do something.

Breaking in to Break Out

A year or so later—I was eleven years old. I was hanging out after dark in front of my house with some older boys when they started talking about how to make some money. We were always foraging through alleys for bottles for the ten-cent refund, and we would also cut the neighbors' grass or shovel snow to make a few bucks. But we were getting older, and our desires were growing. We were always hungry and trying to hustle up enough money to grab Better Made chips, Faygo soda—which we called pop—and the cheap packs of cookies we bought two for a dollar. One of the guys, who we appropriately called Felon, suggested we break into someone's house.

I was terrified by the idea. A few houses had been broken into by the older boys in our neighborhood, and the way our parents talked about it, it sounded horrifying and disrespectful. The rash of burglaries had grown so bad that many of our longtime neighbors had moved away. I will never forget the sadness of seeing a senior couple named Mary and John moving out of their home. There would be no more homemade raisin bread baked by Mary or having our hair tousled by John as he told us stories about the Detroit Tigers legend Ty Cobb. I didn't want to make anyone in our neighborhood feel like that—except for one person: the perverted motherfucker across the street.

The thought of us violating CM's house of horror felt right. I wanted to hurt him bad and let him know that someone in our neighborhood didn't want him there. When I told the fellas that I had a house we should hit, right across the street, they thought I was bullshitting. I told them about the two VCRs and TVs along with CM's musical instruments, and they got excited. "Let's go," one of the boys said before darting across the street; we all followed suit until we were standing on the side of the house, jittery as if we had overdosed on Jolly Ranchers and Now and Laters.

We could tell no one was home. I followed the others around the house as we tried to find a window that wasn't locked. The only one we could open led into the basement. I went in solo, with a plan to go open the door upstairs to let the others in. I had last been inside the house the night of the sleepover. Even though I knew the space well, it all felt strange. Everything in the basement seemed outsized and almost animated with life. I rushed up the stairs to the side door and quickly discovered it needed a key to unlock it from the inside. I ran through the kitchen toward the living room to try the front door, just in time to see a flash of blue and red lights painting the inside of the house.

My little heart was beating like a kick drum. I could hear an officer talking to one of the boys outside and threatening to kick his ass for trying to get into the house. At first, it sounded like the police didn't realize I was inside. I tiptoed into CM's bedroom and climbed under the bed. Even from my hiding spot, I could see out to the driveway and to the flashlights of what seemed like a legion of police surrounding the house.

Soon enough, they knew I was inside and talked to me through the window and told me to open the side door. I told them there was no key in either door. They told me to reach up through the window so they could pull me out. They grabbed my hand and the back of my pants and dragged me through. I had scrapes and bits of glass in my hands but otherwise was no worse for wear.

When my eyes adjusted to the dark, I could see a small gathering of our neighbors standing in front watching. They didn't know the boys I was with, but everyone on the block knew me. I could hear a few neighbors asking "Is that Pumpkin?" my childhood nickname, and saying things like "Boy, you know better" and "I can't believe this." Then I looked up and saw my mother standing there shaking her head. My mother and I had a complex relationship, but despite our struggles, I never wanted to break her heart or embarrass her. I hoped the officer would release me into her custody, but instead, he informed her I had to go to the precinct with the rest of the boys until the homeowner decided whether to press charges.

At the Ninth Precinct, I sat in a glass cell for hours before the officers finally returned with news: CM wasn't pressing charges. They loaded me back into the car and drove me the short distance home.

When we arrived at Felon's house, we were greeted by his mother in a nightgown, screaming at him. As soon as the officers let him out of the car, she began to slap him upside his head as she told him how stupid he was. I began to shake like a soaking wet puppy as I thought about what was going to happen to me when I got home. I anticipated the fiery lash of the belt that I knew was going to tear into my flesh. As we got closer to my house, though, the fear of the ass-whooping shifted to anger. CM was the motherfucker who'd been saved from having his house robbed, and that pissed me off. But as we drove to my punishment, the people I was getting angry at were my parents. They were the adults. They shouldn't have trusted CM to begin with. If they'd protected me, we wouldn't be in this situation.

What's Inside Must Come Out

Decades later, I was sitting in a cell, reading an old journal entry about what I had wanted to do to CM. I felt a deep brooding shame. But with a calm mind, I was now able to offer the little boy inside me a long-needed emotional hug.

I had been intoxicated by anger for most of my life, and now, for the first time, I was coming to terms with the way that anger had allowed me to run away from the truths I needed instead to face head-on. For many years, to my detriment, I used anger to navigate the power dynamics in prison. The angrier I became, the more powerful and less vulnerable I felt. I lay on my bunk, confronting a fear I had long ago buried: the fear of myself and the fear for myself. I was confronting deep shame, fear, and secrets I had held on to for years. I was confronting the broken little boy who had become a broken, angry, and dangerous man.

It was time to face the darkness within and find a way back to the light I once knew as a boy. I had never felt more helpless or hopeless than when I was forced to deal with my own thoughts. Reliving the traumas of my past while grappling with my rage toward CM had left me drained.

I needed a break from reading my journal, so I sought solace in reading passages from a few of the books on my desk, including Plato's *Republic*, before drifting off into a restless dream-filled sleep. In one of the dreams, I found myself in an ancient setting—the Lyceum perhaps—surrounded by men preparing for a heated debate. The environment shifted, and I suddenly stood naked in a small, dark dwelling, face-to-face with my opponent—my angry self. For the first time in my life, it was angry me versus authentic me, my best thoughts of myself versus my worst thoughts of myself. It was war. This dream battle of my past self raging against the new self I was trying to become provided me with two important lessons about life. As long as you have breath in your lungs, you can go back and affirm that innocent kid. And if you are courageous enough to face the worst of who you were, you can become the best version of who you are.

Over the next few days in my cell, pushing through one jagged sentence after another across my notepad, I delved into my past trauma, anger, and violence. As I dug down through those layers in search of my authentic self, what struck me was this: The specifics of our anger don't matter as much as what we choose to do with it. The sources of that anger are often long gone, and we have the power to choose how we respond to their memory.

I had cracked the code and realized I was slowly but surely escaping, liberating myself with wisdom and a testimony that cried out from deep inside of me in the form of the ink that bled out onto the crumpled notepad I held tightly in my hands. For the first time in my prison sentence, I realized my life calling, my raison d'être, was to be free of all of the things that no longer served me or that stood in the way of true happiness.

I realized I had been imprisoned by anger years before the police ever put handcuffs on me. And while I couldn't control when I would be paroled, I now understood I held the keys to my own freedom. It was this awakening that started me on the path to healing.

My family and community culture never encouraged me to be vulnerable with others, and this silence led to a world of hurt for my victim, my family, and myself. For most of my walk of freedom, I had avoided talking to my parents about the anger that drove me to seek revenge, become violent, and serve time in prison. It wasn't until the week of my fiftieth birthday that I began to change that. In separate but equally deep conversations with each of my parents, shit got real.

My anger toward CM was appropriate, but often my rage had me firing at the wrong target. I obtained true freedom by recognizing this and by making decisions that honored my painful past without leaving myself or others in deeper pain. I'd been convicted of violent crimes and served hard time. These facts were and are forever branded to my name, but they don't define all of who I am or have been.

My anger didn't fade with a journal entry or even later with the opening of a cell door. I was finding clarity about the real source of the anger, but it doesn't magically disappear for anyone who has faced trauma—be that sexual assault, child abuse, emotional violence, or disrespect.

Power and control reside in developing tools that help us recognize our triggers. The tools aren't complicated—it's things like journaling, talking to that trusted friend, or taking that drive while listening to a song that lifts your mood. The goal ultimately is to transform the energy of that anger into fuel for self-love, for creation, for action, for reasserting the right thing to do. Or, in my case, do like artist Rakim when he rapped, "I start to think, and then I sink / into the paper, like I was ink."

Turning fifty, I found myself reaching for the familiar and welcoming power of words, but this time instead of writing them down with a makeshift pen, I made those calls to my parents and told them the truth about where it all began. They were devastated, but most importantly, they were present to hear it all.

Drilling Down

If ever there was someone capable of helping you plot and execute your own escape from anger, it would be someone like me. Throughout my youth and young adult years, my anger manifested in many ways: defensiveness, confrontations, an inability to resolve conflicts without violence, shutting down, taking things personally, and resorting to extremes in challenging situations. For a long time, I wore my anger as a protective mask and energizing force, but in fact it was robbing me of joy, happiness, and fulfillment. I thought the mask would keep harmful people away, but instead it ensured that no one could touch my vulnerabilities or establish a deep connection with me. Things began to change as I journaled and eventually asked myself deep and probing questions.

Through journaling, I realized that by acknowledging the painful events of my youth, I could shift the blame back to those who truly harmed me. It took a while, but eventually, I developed true empathy and compassion for the younger me, understanding that I was merely a child, seeking protection, safety, and care.

Through journaling, reading, and meditation, I was finally able to place the blame where it truly belonged.

DIGGING DEEPER

Today I invite you to reflect on these questions: How has anger stood in the way of true happiness? How has it influenced career or business opportunities, friendships, and relationships? How do you see yourself?

These reflections can serve as a guide to understanding your own life: How can you reassign blame appropriately? How can you recognize when anger is locking you into a self-imposed prison?

Liberating yourself from anger doesn't mean you are in denial about its source. But often you need to ferret out anger from its hiding spots, blind spots, and sore spots.

Hiding spots are when anger comes out. When you are short with a colleague, are snippy with your intimate partner, are mean-spirited toward your kids, or lash out at a neighbor who leaves their trash can in front of your driveway, it often means you're using the anger to hide from something.

Blind spots are when you aren't even aware of what is happening inside you when the smallest thing sets you off. You may not even be truly aware of the source of this rage.

Sore spots are those areas of your life where your anger is easily triggered when an old pain flares. Getting underneath the emotion in these moments is when you have the greatest opportunity to break free.

 **KEYS TO RELEASING ANGER**

1. Write Down Your Anger
When you find yourself in the grip of anger, take a moment to put your feelings on paper or on your phone or laptop. Write down what specifically is causing you to feel this way. Later, when the intensity has subsided, revisit what you wrote. What I discovered for myself was that it was both old and new shit but mostly old shit that had me locked into anger.

2. Identify the Primary Emotion
Be patient with yourself and dig deeper. Anger often masks other emotions such as shame, sadness, fear, or frustration. Try to identify what's beneath the surface of anger. What I learned was that it was never the person cutting me off in traffic or the rude service person; it was always something deeper in my past.

3. Create a Countermantra
Craft a mantra that counters the negative aspects of anger. "This anger doesn't serve my higher good, it doesn't optimize my potential, and it doesn't add value to the life I am worthy of." Repeating this mantra can help shift your perspective.

4. Meditate to Release Anger
Conquering anger involves acknowledging it, understanding its underlying causes, and actively working to counter it with positive affirmations and calming practices like meditation. These steps allow you to transform your relationship with anger and find healthier ways to manage and release it.

Meditation can help you calm your mind, gain perspective, and release the intense emotions associated with anger. Practice meditation until you feel the angry energy dissipating. If you are having trouble getting started, I highly recommend you check out *The Miracle of Mindfulness* by Thich Nhat Hanh: "Mindfulness is the miracle by which we master and restore ourselves."

CHAPTER THREE
SHAME

> I can be changed by what happens to me, but I refuse to be reduced by it.
>
> —Maya Angelou, *Letter to My Daughter*

Standing in my parents' living room on Ferguson Street, I watched what felt like an endless stream of people flowing in and out of the house. My parents sat at the dining room table, where they had sat for decades when company came by. It was the place where we watched the game or listened to my dad pontificate about life. It was where we played music and spades, where we laughed and joked, and where people now sat with tears in their eyes. Although I was surrounded by family and friends, I felt something inside me breaking and something deeper breaking open. This wasn't just grief or anger—it was deeper, heavier. It was a shame, a weight I had carried for years but never named. As we laid Sherrod to rest, I realized I wasn't just mourning his death—I was mourning a part of myself that I had buried in a prison cell many years before.

On the flight back to LA, the weight of shame sat on my chest like extra baggage I couldn't check at the gate. Shame I carried from childhood, through prison, and now as a big brother who couldn't save his little brother.

If I was going to be free, I had to unpack that shame and its roots.

On the surface, there was anger and grief but also something else, something more. Guilt had been my go-to for years, my default emotion. Even though I had been forgiven and had forgiven myself, there were moments when guilt would rise from my gut and spill over into my life. So over the next few months, as I sat at home and at work, labeling what I was feeling as guilt felt logical, practical, and easy.

I asked myself, "Is this my karma? Is this what I get for my past? Is this our family's chickens coming home to roost?" Questioning myself while watching my family grieve brought me to the edge, but what really broke me was the sadness in my stepmother's eyes. That's when I realized it wasn't just guilt I was feeling—it was shame. I didn't feel worthy of being in the room, shedding tears with my loved ones, or consoling anyone. It was suffocating. And it wasn't just about Sherrod. It was about everything. Sitting there and looking into her eyes, into my dad's eyes, into Sherrod's dad's eyes, I felt indicted. I had to get up and go outside to breathe, just breathe.

When I stepped out the front door, a few of the younger members of my family and some of our friends swarmed around me with hugs and consoling words, but I couldn't fully receive them. I was too deep into feeling like I didn't deserve their love and concern. That's the thing about shame: it gets so deep inside you, you can't appreciate the fullness of what's happening outside of you. It wasn't the first time I had felt shame, but now I felt I couldn't escape. That sense that my life would always be marred by my past was the essence of being locked into the shame cage.

That shame took me back to CM's bedroom, to the first time I learned to hide behind anger and guilt. As a young boy unable to speak up, to name the danger I was in, feeling shame for being preyed on by someone I trusted, I felt like something was wrong with me. Before I got out of prison, I thought I could save everyone in my family and neighborhood from the things I had gone through. I thought the letters I sent home sharing my experience and the cautionary phone calls would get the job done until I could be there in person. I thought I had wisdom from my experience on the streets, credibility from surviving prison, and the respect that comes with getting out and staying out. But that's not how life works. I realized I didn't have the power to change the outcome for Sherrod any more than I had been able to for my cousin who, in a challenging moment, took his own life; for my niece, who got caught up with a boyfriend and ended up in prison; or for my four nephews, who all landed in prison as well.

Grief and shame trigger the what-ifs and provide the magical notion that we can somehow control someone else's life choices or outcomes. Those what-ifs are like the bars of the cell: We tell ourselves bullshit stories, we villainize ourselves, and we try to award ourselves power that we cannot possess.

The truth? I couldn't save my brother, nor anyone else, and as a kid, I damn sure couldn't have known that CM was a pedophile.

I could caution, warn, and advise, but I was not the puppet master controlling the actors. However, I did have the power to liberate myself from the damning all-encompassing feeling of shame. As Friedrich Nietzsche said, "What is the seal of liberation? No longer being ashamed in front of oneself."

When I was thirty, still in solitary confinement and journaling as a way to chart a path forward, I wrote this:

> I'm really struggling with an internal conflict, and it feels like I'm losing the battle. I'm letting negativity take root in my heart, and this prison is seeping into my pores. I miss my old self. I want to laugh again. My thoughts have become so negative, I can't believe they're mine. I don't know how I got here—how I can't imagine anything positive happening for me without something negative creeping in. I want to believe there's something good in my future, but the more I try to believe, the more the negative shows up. I can't keep living with these thoughts.

When I left prison, I truly thought I had moved on from the anger and the guilt, but when Sherrod died, something inside me snapped. I had moved past guilt, but the anger and shame still clung to me like a shadow.

Every time I shared my story or truth—in interviews or with friends or lovers—I felt like I was being dragged back into that prison cell, defined by my worst moment. My past had been weaponized against me in concrete ways more times than I could count. In interviews, I was antagonized. In relationships I was reminded that I had murdered a man. And every time I filled out an application and checked the box that asked if I had a felony, I was brought back to 1991. Each time, I felt smaller, more broken. It was easy to tell the world that we shouldn't be defined by our worst moments, but when the world kept doing just that, it was hard not to believe it. While I hadn't physically recidivated, I found myself returning to an emotional prison I'd thought was in my past. I knew I had to find a new way out, and as with any great escape plan, I needed support.

Finding support in books and the stories of others had helped me break through when I was in a prison cell. This time, as I searched to better understand shame, Brené Brown's name and book, *Daring Greatly*, kept coming up. Like millions of people, I watched her TED Talk and listened to her interviews. We were practically besties—or at least that's what I liked to joke. Sure, her TED Talk had twenty million more views than mine, but we'd both written books, so in my head, that made us twins—except, you know, for the obvious differences. I dove headfirst into her book, but the deeper I got into her work on shame, the more I started to resent it. It was pushing me in ways that felt exhausting.

I was tired: Tired of telling my story repeatedly. Tired of searching for a way out of the deep shit through stories that had torn me to shreds. Each time I thought I'd made progress, something would pull me back. A news headline—boom, a trigger. A conversation with a stranger—trigger. Filling out a job application—trigger. Even something like travel—trigger. And there it was again, over and over. But I knew I had to trust Brené and her brilliant work. I mean, if Oprah Winfrey and millions of people across the world trusted her, who was I not to?

Brené outlined four key pillars of shame resilience: recognizing shame and understanding its triggers, practicing critical awareness, reaching out for support, and speaking about shame. Sounds simple enough, right? But shame had been running wild in my life for so long that I couldn't even see it for what it was. It didn't show up in neat little boxes like she described. I put *Daring Greatly* down, made up narratives of why it didn't apply to me, and generally just called bullshit on her, more times than I care to remember. But I kept coming back. Then one day, her definition of shame hit me like a George Foreman punch: Shame is negative self-evaluation, believing there's something inherently wrong with you. Damn. Negative self-evaluation. Believing something was wrong with me. Brené had helped me crack the code.

That's what I had been doing all along without even realizing it. Every time I looked at my family, every time I got into a heated argument with someone I loved, I was reliving that same shame. I had convinced myself that something was wrong with me, and I had to show people that I was OK, I wasn't a threat, and I was a good human being. I was overcompensating, trying to prove I wasn't some monster. But at the same time, I couldn't fully absolve myself for the things I'd done. It was madness. A sickness. A prison of its own.

I let family members and friends use my past as a weapon. I let colleagues exploit my story, my insights, and my brilliance for their own gain. All in the name of trying to be accepted, to feel "normal." I stayed in relationships long after their expiration date because I thought it was my responsibility to make others feel whole—even when I wasn't whole myself.

That money you lend to a family member that's never paid back. That insight you share with a coworker that gets used in a big meeting while your name is never mentioned. That was me—the guilt, shame, and desperate need to be seen as normal let me justify other people's actions that caused me harm. Personally and professionally, I was living in a mental prison as brutal as any cell I'd ever been in.

But here's the thing that hit the hardest: This feeling wasn't new. As a kid, I was often the butt of jokes from the older homies after my family broke apart. I roamed the neighborhood, a runaway youth, long before I was seduced by the drug trade. I felt shame from things large and small, like that time I ripped the seat of my pants climbing a neighbor's garage and had to walk down the street with kids laughing at me. My friends thought it was hilarious, but I felt embarrassed as hell, trying to cover my torn pants with my tiny hands. I was ashamed of my parents' divorce and the times when we had to rely on government-issued food because coming from a broken home and poverty meant you were less than.

One memory surfaced in my mind when I started doing the deep work around my shame. We were standing outside Denby High School on the east side of Detroit, an assortment of teenagers clad in Fila and Adidas tracksuits. Hip-hop was still finding its identity, and we were in the middle of one of our first ciphers. I'll never forget hearing someone shout from the back, "He's biting, he's biting!" I spun around, expecting to see someone chomping on another kid's arm or leg. But instead, a finger pointed at one of the boys who had everyone gathered around. "You stole those rhymes from Chaucer. Those aren't yours." The boy tried to deny it at first, but before he could get the words out, other kids chimed in.

I think I remember that moment so clearly for two reasons. First, the series of emotions that flashed across the kid's face—from shock to embarrassment to what I now recognize as deep shame. I felt bad for him. And second, it baffled me that someone would want to claim someone else's story so badly, they'd steal it and present it as their own. Yet we've all done it—posing as someone we want to be instead of who we are. I imagined I was a basketball player every time I tossed a piece of paper into a wastebasket. I also imagined who I'd be without the conviction, without the guilt, without the shame. I was fighting against the narratives forced on me, but I was also trapped by the ones I had built in my own mind. My shame had me believing narratives about me that simply weren't true. I had taken chunks out of my own identity, swallowing stories and lies that weren't mine, ideas that caused me harm.

I knew then that if I didn't break free from this shame, I'd never live up to my dreams of being a good father, a good husband, a good human being. I had to reclaim my story. I wasn't just a boy with a gun. I wasn't the worst thing I had ever done. I was a man who had made terrible mistakes, but I had also worked to apologize, to atone. I was a man of my word, a man who had built a family, a career, and a life worth living. I also wasn't a bad kid who tried to burglarize CM's house; I was a kid who was angry at an adult who tried to sexually assault him.

In 1961, Carl Rogers gave us one of the keys to breaking free in his book *On Becoming a Person: A Therapist's View of Psychotherapy*. Rogers doesn't just explore the mind—he digs deep into the heart of what it means to be personally free, be self-accepting, and live with authenticity. His message? You've got to fully accept yourself—flaws, scars, mistakes, all of it—before real growth can happen. Freeing myself from shame came not from *resisting* who I am holistically but from embracing it. As Rogers said, "The curious paradox is that when I accept myself just as I am, then I can change."

Those words coursed through me like the waters of the Nile, as if they had always been meant for me. And even years later, they still ring true. Today, I realize this war I was fighting wasn't just about freeing myself from guilt, anger, and shame. It was a battle for my soul. It was about whether I could make peace with my past and still have the courage to build a future. Could I sit with the darkest parts of my story and still find light on the other side? That's Rogers's message: transformation through radical self-acceptance. It's the hardest fight any of us will ever face.

This wasn't about shedding my identity as a convicted murderer or embracing a different one as a writer. It was about rejecting the emotional responses to trauma that were keeping me locked in a version of myself I no longer wanted to be. We're all imprisoned in some way. We all have our hidden prisons. We cling to what's familiar, even when it's harmful, because we're afraid of the unknown. But true freedom means questioning those old beliefs, rejecting the outdated narratives, and creating a new identity.

When I failed at something, it used to eat me alive. Missing deadlines when I worked at the *Michigan Citizen*, fumbling words on the stage, unintentionally hurting a loved one's feelings—it made me feel hopeless, like I couldn't get anything right. That's what shame does. It blinds you and binds you. It keeps you from seeing all the times you did get it right, all the moments when you showed up for yourself and others. Shame erases your wins, both big and small. But those victories are real. You've got to fight for and hold on to them.

Every time I visit a prison and stand in front of men and women still locked inside those walls, I'm reminded of how far I've come. I'm reminded that the more freedom I claim for myself, the more impact my work will have in helping them find their own way out. But I'm also reminded of how easy it is to slip back literally and figuratively. The mental prison is always waiting, but now I know I have the keys to break free.

One of the things I also learned from journaling is the power of going back and reassigning the proper emotions to past experiences. I remember once, when I was a kid, one of the older homies telling me "Your daddy is gonna whoop your ass" as he looked down at the wreckage of vinyl records scattered all over the sidewalk and street. I had taken stacks of my dad's prized records outside, and we launched them across the neighborhood like frisbees, laughing, completely oblivious to their real value. When my dad found out, he didn't yell at first—he just looked at me with something in his eyes that hit differently. Yeah, he was mad, but there was something else—something deeper. I couldn't put words to it then, but I could feel it, right in my chest. I think that's one of the moments when I felt shame. The look in my dad's eyes told me that those records had value well beyond their price. For years that look haunted me.

Behind my dad's anger, there was sadness. I had broken something that meant more to him than I could understand. He wasn't just mad about some records—he was hurt.

My dad loved music. Lived for it. Collecting those records was his pride. He grounded me, kept me inside while my friends played outside. But honestly, the real punishment was the shame I felt—shame in hurting him in a way I hadn't even realized I could and depriving him of something I couldn't replace.

But here's what made the difference: My dad didn't let that shame fester. He sat me down and talked it out—explained why it mattered, why breaking other people's things wasn't just about the stuff but about respecting what they valued. He knew I didn't fully understand what those records meant to him, but he took the time to explain, and he gave me space to try to understand and grow instead of letting that shame define me.

But I still managed to carry that moment with me into my incarceration. Shame wasn't new to me, but prison worked it into deep grooves. From being told to bend and spread my ass cheeks during strip searches to being denied food, there was a litany of daily shame-inducing assaults. There was the time an officer wouldn't let me head to the showers because I didn't own a pair of the specific cheap tan shower shoes we were supposed to have. I tried to get by with my regular shoes, but the officer coldly cut me off, saying the only alternative was to go barefoot in that grimy, disease-ridden shower where thirty men had just gone through. I let that shame curl up into something darker: anger. I was mad at the officer for how she treated me, but mostly, I was mad at myself. I had been a drug dealer on the street, I had a family with jobs and friends who hustled, but I didn't have two dollars to purchase shower shoes. That tiny moment of powerlessness caused me to shrink inward.

Here's the thing about shame: It doesn't always come from the worst things we've done or the worst things done to us. Sometimes, it shows up in quiet moments when we're faced with our own humanity, when a small indignity chips away at our pride and uncovers the rawness of our pasts, something painful, something vulnerable.

There was a moment like this at work I'll never forget. I was one of the only men I knew convicted of a serious crime who had risen to the rank of C-suite executive. We were just months away from launching the rebrand. I was the vice president of corporate communications of a company valued at nine billion dollars that was changing its name from TripActions to Navan. I was responsible for taking an existing video project and turning it into something the sales team could use to sell our product. The video had to shift from the usual corporate style to something more people centered. I was hyped. This was my moment to do what I knew I did well: I was a master storyteller and had a knack for connecting with people on an emotional level. This should have been a lay-up.

I dove in with the production team we'd hired, covering the budget, deliverables—everything that came with a project of this size. There was pressure, sure, but I was ready. I put together a storyboard, sent out my instructions, and waited for the team to deliver an Emmy-worthy video.

Then the first draft came back, and it wasn't what I had envisioned. The video was dark, which should have been the first red flag. It was missing that warm, vibrant, people-first vibe that reflected our new brand identity, and it wasn't what I was aiming for. I raised my concerns while trying to encourage the team: "Can you lighten this up in post and give it some swagger?" They assured me they could. And I trusted them. As a creative myself, I knew what it meant to be trusted with a vision and project of this magnitude. I wasn't just thinking of the bottom line; I was also thinking of the people on the team.

But here's where I messed up: Instead of leaning into my business side—the part that knew I should have given more detailed direction and been more clear with my expectations—I stayed in my creative lane. When the second draft came back and it was still dark, I didn't push back or scrap that version altogether. I trusted them again. And when the final version was delivered, it was a disaster. It felt like a poorly executed high school project—nowhere near what we needed for the rebrand.

When the CEO confronted me about it, my ego was bruised, and I felt the ugly shadow of shame. He didn't tear me down; he simply told me to find another vendor and get the job done. So I did. I reached out to friends in the creative space, and together we produced a beautiful, elegant video that hit all the right notes. But the damage had been done. I had blown the budget. I had failed on my first big project, and I carried the weight of that failure deep inside me for the next couple of weeks. It was hard for me to lean into the excitement and all the festivities of the rebrand even though I was leading all the communications around it.

After the debacle with the video, the CEO and I sat down for our next one-on-one. He walked me through a process he had introduced me to that was similar to a military after-action report—it was an unflinching, methodical approach to dissecting failure. It was supposed to be purely analytical, free of emotion, focused only on learning and course correction. But as we moved through the questions, I couldn't ignore the sinking weight of shame settling in.

1. *What went wrong?* I forced myself to lay out the missteps, but each one felt like a blow, a reminder of what I should have done differently.
2. *Why did it go wrong?* The gaps in execution, the overlooked details—I saw them all, and it was hard not to take it personally. The process demanded detachment, but my mind clung to the failure like it was a reflection of my own inadequacy.
3. *What can we do differently next time?* This was meant to be the productive part, the moment to pivot toward

solutions. But even as we mapped out adjustments, I was still wrestling with the discomfort of having fallen short.

The process wasn't about blame, yet I felt its weight. It was meant to be emotionless, yet I found myself wading through emotions I hadn't expected—shame, frustration, the haunting feeling that I should have done better. And maybe that was part of the process too—not just analyzing failure but learning how to sit with it, own it, and move forward anyway.

But at that moment, I felt ashamed. It wasn't just about messing up the video—it brought up all these other moments where I felt like I wasn't good enough, like I hadn't done enough. And that's the thing about shame. It's not about the specific mistake you make—it's about all the unresolved pain you carry from your past. Shame doesn't just live in the present moment; it drags the past into your present, making you feel like every failure is proof that you're not built for success or worthy of love and joy.

I could've just accepted the feedback, acknowledged that I had messed up, and moved on. But instead, I started beating myself up. Work no longer felt enjoyable. I felt like I was constantly being tested, like every moment was another opportunity to fail. But the truth is, the only test happening was in my head. That internal voice kept telling me, "You're not built for this grind. You're not good enough to be in corporate America. You can't handle feedback because it brings up all your old shit."

Then I caught myself: I realized I had to do more internal work. I had to get down to the truth of why these old wounds kept haunting me. On my flight home from our office in Palo Alto, I wrote a note to myself that said, "You may not always get it right, you may not succeed at everything you put your energy into, and you may stumble along on your journey, but if you dare to examine the whole truth of who you are, you will walk away from each moment not with the bruise of shame but with a lesson that you have fought so hard to heal. You are an extraordinary storyteller, creator, and leader. In fact, you are a bad motherfucker. After all, not everyone can pull themselves up from the dregs of society to the C suite."

DIGGING DEEPER

What are the things that make you feel unworthy? What are those things that make you slink back into old ideas of the self that no longer exist? Maybe it's the sting of abuse or the weight of being embarrassed again and again. Some carry the shame of not standing up for themselves. But here's the truth: Standing up for yourself starts with believing you're worth the fight. It's knowing, deep down, that you're lovable, worthy of respect, and deserving of dignity.

Reflection Exercise: My invitation for you is to write down five major moments when you allowed shame to hide your authentic self. When you finish your list, go back and read each line and apologize to yourself for the moments you allowed a shameful narrative to take root and for the times you denied yourself the freedom to be a human being.

Place this document in an envelope and seal it. Place the envelope in a safe place, and wait one year from the day you finish it to open and read it. While we are on our healing journey, it's important for us to go back and remind ourselves of how far we have come.

 KEYS TO RELEASING SHAME

1. Speak Your Truth
- Shame thrives in silence and secrecy. Find safe spaces and trusted people with whom you can share your authentic experiences.
- Your story has power, and speaking it out loud begins to break shame's hold.
- Remember that vulnerability isn't weakness—it's the courage to be seen as you truly are.

2. Challenge Shame-Based Thoughts
- When shame whispers "You're not good enough" or "You don't belong," recognize these are thoughts, not truths.
- Ask yourself, "Who defined these standards? Are they really mine?"
- Question the assumptions behind your shame, and consider where these beliefs originated.

3. Reclaim Your Narrative
- Your past doesn't define your path. Take ownership of how you interpret and frame your experiences.
- Write a new narrative that acknowledges your challenges but emphasizes your resilience, growth, and inherent worthiness.

PART 2

FINDING YOUR STRENGTH

CHAPTER FOUR
VULNERABILITY

> Vulnerability is our most accurate measure of courage.
>
> —Brené Brown, TED Talk

I tapped "Home" on my phone—the contact tied to our family's number since 1986. "Hey, Blood," my dad answered, using a greeting common among the Black men who fought for the country during the Vietnam War. "Hey, Pops," I responded.

Vulnerability is something I've always had to grapple with, whether it was the kind of vulnerability that came with hustling in the streets of Detroit or simply growing up in prison as a youth.

But there's another kind of vulnerability—the kind that comes from feeling and embracing emotions, even when they're uncomfortable. Some of the most important steps in my own development have come from breaking through emotional barriers built up between me and my parents, something I started to do in deeply personal and vulnerable conversations I had with each of them as we all recovered from Sherrod's death.

My mom and dad came from a generation that kept everything close to the chest, rarely opening up to their children. I, too, had held in so much over the years, but to move forward, I knew we finally had to share more.

During one call, I told my pops that I was working on understanding my childhood. He loves a good conversation, and one of his favorite subjects is family. He loves to tell us stories about aunts, uncles, and cousins from Mississippi, most of whom I don't know or whom I only vaguely remember. Growing up, we didn't spend as much time with my pop's extended family as I did with my mother's side, but he always made sure I knew their names and faces the best he could.

As generous a storyteller as he'd been in the past, I was now asking for more. "Pops, what was your dream for me when you knew I was going to be born?"

I wanted to know who they were as young parents in 1972. I was curious about their world—what their lives looked like, what dreams they had for themselves and for me, and how the events of the times shaped their hopes for my future.

My dad was twenty-five, my mom twenty-three. I was my mother's fourth child and my father's first. I imagined what it must have been like for them, raising kids and navigating life as a young, married couple in Detroit during such a turbulent era. The year I was born, Richard Nixon was president, and the Vietnam War was still raging. The Watergate scandal was dominating political discussions and eroding public trust in the government. Two months after my birth, the Munich Olympics were overshadowed by tragedy. It was a time of political upheaval and social change. How did my parents make sense of the world, and how did they envision my future in it?

Amid the turmoil, there was hope too. Music and culture were flourishing. Al Green's *Let's Stay Together* and Don McLean's *American Pie* were top-ten albums that year, and Roberta Flack's "The First Time Ever I Saw Your Face" topped the singles chart. *The Godfather*, one of the greatest movies about family, redefined cinema. Imagining my parents and their lives back then, I flashed back to a photo of my dad donning his Air Force uniform and an afro and a picture of my mother in a pretty dress with her pregnant belly. I was eager to hear how, if any, these moments, these cultural shifts, played a part in the dreams they had for me.

Who were James and Arlene White in 1972? Like so many of their generation, they were trying to settle down and establish a life for themselves as a young married couple, homeowners, and parents. Over the years, both my parents had told me, in their own ways, that they were striving for their slice of the American dream. The house, the dogs, the jobs, and social status. But I often found myself wondering, Where did I fit into that dream?

I asked my father about his own upbringing. He told me how his father was the primary cook in their family. He talked about the incredible soul food my grandfather whipped up for his family. I pictured my grandfather's pecan-colored skin as he stood in the kitchen. I imagined the aroma of collard greens, fried chicken, and macaroni and cheese. My dad told me stories of playing baseball with the other kids in the neighborhood;

about getting in trouble hanging with my uncle John, who my dad described as a rabble-rouser; about his choice to go down the straight and narrow because he didn't like getting whoopings or being punished.

My pops told me he knew from the moment I was born that I was meant for something special in the world. "Son, even though your life has had some ups and downs, I knew you were going to help people. I didn't know when or how, I just always knew it. I never let go of that dream for you and probably saw it before you did. Remember all of those letters you used to send me from prison? Well, if I never said this, I want you to know that those letters saved your old man more than once."

The warmth of that conversation finally liberated the little boy inside me who had been carrying a burden for far too long. I finally felt ready for what I knew would be the toughest conversation I'd ever had with my dad. It was time to share the weight of the secret I'd carried with me for so long, a weight that almost killed me.

I dreaded it, and it took me a while to get there. For a few nights leading up to the conversation, I had put myself in his shoes and played the scenario out in my head as I thought he'd receive it. As a father myself, I understood how difficult it would be for him to hear that he hadn't been able to protect me from CM. I didn't want him to think I was blaming him. My goal was to approach the conversation in a way that would bring us closer.

I didn't want my father's heart to break, but I needed him to understand why I had broken into that man's house all those years before. That act of rebellion wasn't just revenge—it was a cry for help. It was a symptom of something deeper. For years, I had beaten myself up for being a "bad" kid, but as I'd worked through the layers, I'd realized I wasn't bad. I was a kid who had encountered bad adults. And as that realization took root, it opened pathways for me to grow into a full understanding of personal agency. For years I had blamed myself and believed that something was wrong with me instead of realizing that something was wrong with CM.

This is the reality for so many who have been traumatized. We internalize it, blaming ourselves instead of the adults or people who harmed us.

"Pops, CM tried to molest me, and that was the reason I broke into his house. I wanted to hurt him the way he tried to hurt me," I said. There was a moment of silence that hung between us like a sheet on a clothing line.

My dad listened quietly as I shared what happened on that night long ago at CM's. When he finally spoke, his voice cracked as he apologized for not digging deeper into why I had done what I had. "Son, I am so sorry that happened to you," he said with a hitch in his voice. He told me that he knew back then that there had to be something more to the story, but he'd never known I was fighting back the only way I knew how.

We talked some more, and when we finally got off the phone, I was spent. I lay down on the couch and drifted off to sleep. While our conversation had been heavy, I came away feeling lighter. Vulnerability didn't just help me heal—it allowed me to connect with my dad in ways I never thought possible.

Later, I called my mother. We'd never had the best relationship, but we had started putting the effort and energy into healing. I was determined to forge a deeper connection, and I decided the way to do it was by interviewing her about my entry into the world. I told her that she didn't have to share anything she didn't want to or anything that made her uncomfortable. More than anything, I wanted her to know that I was there to understand and learn and not to judge. To my shock and excitement, my mother told me I could ask her anything because she was an open book. My mother's willingness to be present and share her dreams for me, along with her own dreams and stories, was beautiful and affirming. Knowing how difficult it had to be for her to be vulnerable. I felt blessed.

My mother has a beautiful Midwestern drawl, laughs easily, and has an innocence about her that emerges every now and then. During the call, she shared things I had never known about her childhood. She told me about the abuse she endured as a young girl, the pain of being neglected and abandoned. She opened up about the assaults on her body, the great deal of pressure she felt she was under from the time she was a teenager. Her story hit me hard because I realized that I had carried similar feelings when I was out in the streets, feeling isolated and unloved. I started to see more of the little girl who had just wanted to be loved and protected in the same way I had yearned for safety and acceptance as a kid. I was reminded of something Oprah Winfrey said during a conversation with Dr. Bruce Perry while talking about her own mother: "She did the best that she knew." Like Oprah's mother, my mother did the best she knew.

Once I told her what happened to me, she said, "I'm sorry, Pumpkin. I wish that had never happened." We sat in silence as we both gathered ourselves. She then told me stories about me being a funny baby and a smart little boy. She told me that there were times she was afraid for me and my siblings because she knew we were growing up in a world that could be cruel and where Black boys ended up dead or in prison.

I thought about both of my parents confronting their own sense of being, surviving the uncertainty of the times, and trying to raise children.

My father, too, knew the struggles of working in a world where overt racism was a daily reality, and the pressure of providing for his family weighed on him constantly. He joined the Air Force in 1964 at just seventeen.

When I asked my dad about that era and what he thought, he shared a perspective we don't often hear: "Yes, son, there were some racists, but they were the minority—and they've always been the minority. For the most part, the people I worked alongside were good people who just wanted to serve their country."

When I asked my mother if she had ever feared for my dad's safety, she told me there wasn't a night in those early years when she didn't breathe a sigh of relief the moment he walked through the door. But as time went on, things started to change.

These are the burdens that so many parents carry silently. It was heavy hearing their stories, but they also resonated with my own. Locking away our pain and fears only imprisons us and threatens to destroy us from the inside out. Vulnerability was the antidote. As we opened up, something powerful happened. It wasn't just healing—it was a release. By sharing our own struggles, we each gave the other permission to share their traumas, triumphs, failures, and dreams.

When I asked my dad what he thought about the times he grew up in, he said, "Son, it was tough. After my dad moved out, I had to figure out what it meant to be a man. The lessons I needed to know about being a father weren't there, so I had to figure it all out on my own." Up until the conversation, I'd never even known my grandfather had moved out or why.

Hearing my father talk about his own life made me realize just how many men feel they can't afford to show weakness or open up and the resentment and pain that creates. I have also seen this play out with CEOs, business leaders, and coaches who hide behind the facade of toughness. When we allow ourselves to open up, to be vulnerable, we can start to take control of our narrative. We can stop letting shame and fear define us, and we empower those around us to do the same.

Hearing my mother's story of being violated and assaulted brought home why so many women in my life say they don't feel safe in a world full of men. It also reminded me of something many women had shared on social media. When asked if they would prefer to be stranded in the woods with a bear or a man who was a stranger, overwhelmingly, women chose the bear.

In those conversations with my parents, we covered so much that had gone unsaid for so long—their broken promises, their dreams, their joys, and their heartbreaks. It was painful to hear my father's sorrow over my incarceration and to know how many sleepless nights my mother spent worrying about me. Though they had shared some of their heartbreak while I was in prison, it was hitting me differently as a middle-aged man, listening to my aging parents.

I once facilitated a group discussion around a book called *Houses of Healing*. I had started the group class after discovering a box of books in the back of the library where I worked alongside my friend Calvin. After reading the book, I asked the librarian if I could run the class. In a matter of weeks, we went from a small group to standing room only. I watched grown men crack open for the first time, shedding tears they had stored up for years and sometimes decades. That class empowered me to think about the liberating force that was created by laying bare the things we held inside. But it also showed me that vulnerability wasn't just about stilling yourself for potential assaults or shedding tears with your fellow man; it was so much more.

The power of vulnerability was encoded in daring to be greater than your circumstances by taking your destiny into your own hands. To make it through the trauma and out of prison, I had to be vulnerable enough to believe in myself long before anyone else did. Who would have thought I'd achieve the things I have—the mental clarity, the spiritual grit, or the enduring vision? Or that I would receive the proverbial cherries on top: the awards, the accolades, the money, the life I'm living now? None of it came easy, and all of it required an emotional muscle I didn't know I had until I decided to claim a new way of seeing life.

Opening oneself up is different from simply identifying emotional triggers. It's about stepping into your truth, no matter how raw or uncertain it feels. Vulnerability forces you to use your imagination to create a new way of seeing life. It's the foundation for healing because, as I've learned, you can't heal what you don't reveal. It's getting real and raw with yourself. It's more than being honest; it's accepting unchangeable facts and saying I will no longer allow these things to define or confine me.

I've also seen firsthand the power of vulnerability in a business context. For years, I worked at Navan under CEO Ariel Cohen. Navan is in the business of helping companies manage their travel bookings and expenses, so when the world stopped traveling, during COVID that was a serious challenge. Ariel responded by bringing the whole leadership team together for a series of offsites where we spent time getting real about the state of our company. We read books together and had one-on-ones with him. This deepened our trust in the company and bolstered our confidence that we would come out on the other side better than before. Indeed, we did: Navan went from a pre-COVID valuation of four billion dollars to a post-COVID valuation of over nine billion. The kind of vulnerability that our CEO modeled made all of us stronger.

Great leaders aren't the ones who always have the answers—they're the ones who get real. The best leaders are those who remain open and transparent, even when things aren't going perfectly. They are the ones who engage with their employees at a human level and who look for help from those with different experiences and perspectives. Think of the CEOs who had to lay off employees during the pandemic. The great ones held all-hands meetings, got direct, and provided context. The not-so-great ones hit send on impersonal emails and let HR handle the rest. Great leaders show up in tough moments, admit when they're struggling, and connect emotionally with their teams.

Vulnerability isn't a weakness—it's the key to becoming the best version of yourself. It allows you to show up fully in every part of your life. It lets you stop performing and start living. In the corporate world, vulnerability builds trust. It creates an environment where people feel safe to take risks, to be creative, and to grow. When leaders are vulnerable, they create a culture where everyone can be real, where failure is a learning opportunity, not a source of shame.

At Navan, I once invited the executive leadership team to the Ole Skool Cafe, a restaurant in San Francisco staffed entirely by individuals who had been incarcerated. I was nervous about bringing colleagues into that space. I was worried about being judged, but I knew it was vital to connect our company to the work we said we cared about. To my relief, my colleagues showed up with open minds, and we had an incredible experience that deepened our shared commitment. We enjoyed succulent beef short ribs, fried catfish, and creamy mac and cheese over drinks and laughs. They connected with the young hostess and chefs. My goal was to show my team why it was important that we give people second chances and why it's important to find talent in unconventional ways. After that outing, our company reimagined how we processed background searches that came back negative. Instead of tossing those résumés out, we probed further and interviewed people with felonies the same way we interviewed other candidates, and that led us to consider hiring people we never would have before.

In my journey, I've experienced the transformative power of vulnerability as an employee and as a leader, a son, and a parent.

When kids feel safe, when they know they can come to you without judgment, it changes everything. It protects them inside and out because they know they have a safe space to say, "Hey, this doesn't feel right." The same can be said for employees and colleagues.

I've created that space for my son. He knows he can come to me with anything. If I say something too harsh, he can call me out. He'll say, "Dad, that didn't feel good." That's something I couldn't have imagined growing up, and it wouldn't have been possible if I hadn't first broken free from my own shame. Learning to embrace vulnerability with my parents made it possible to be the father, the man, and the husband I am today.

Vulnerability has taught me it's OK to stumble—whether as a leader, a parent, or a spouse. None of these roles require having all the answers, but they do require authenticity, especially when things go wrong. Embracing that lesson transformed my relationships with colleagues and teams, fostering trust, which is the foundation of every successful partnership. In my personal life, it was breaking down on a call to my friend Fame while on my way to the hospital where Sekou lay in bed. Vulnerability, in that moment, wasn't weakness—it was a bridge to connection and support when I needed it. In prison it was talking to my friend Calvin every day about my dreams as a writer. In that moment, I wasn't just talking about wild dreams; I was having my thoughts affirmed by a friend.

The most profound lesson vulnerability taught me, in my personal and professional life, is this: When you get real, when you drop the armor, you create space for others to do the same. That's where healing happens. That's where real connection and growth begin. Whether in the boardroom or the living room, vulnerability is what makes us human. It's the key to leading, loving, and living with purpose.

At first, vulnerability feels like a risk, like stepping onto unstable ground with no guarantee that it will hold. But what I've found is that the moment we stop holding our stories hostage, we stop being held hostage by them. That's the paradox of vulnerability: What we fear will break us is often what sets us free.

Maya Angelou knew this truth intimately. When she was first asked to write *I Know Why the Caged Bird Sings*, she hesitated. She feared what it would mean to lay her story bare—the trauma, the struggles, the moments of deepest pain. Would people judge her? Would speaking it aloud make it more real?

But she did it anyway. She wrote. She told her truth. And in doing so, she not only freed herself but gave voice to millions who had felt trapped by their own untold stories. She later wrote, "There is no greater agony than bearing an untold story inside you."

That's the lesson. Vulnerability isn't just about exposure—it's about release. It's about stepping into the light of our own truth and realizing that no matter how heavy our stories feel, they become lighter the moment we share them.

The most important conversations I've ever had weren't with my parents or anyone else. They were with me. And those are often the hardest conversations to face. Vulnerability became the force that allowed me to confront my deepest fears, especially the self-accusing spirit within me—the part that had been cloaked in shame and humiliation for years. Opening up to vulnerability wasn't just an emotional tool—it was a pathway to freedom.

DIGGING DEEPER

As you move forward, I challenge you: What are the stories you're still carrying that need to be freed? What truths are you holding back that could be the keys to your liberation?

Vulnerability is not just about admitting our fears—it's about walking through them and coming out the other side stronger, freer, and more fully ourselves.

Here are some areas to reflect on:
- **In professional settings**, reflect on how authenticity could strengthen your leadership or teamwork. When have you seen vulnerability create trust in the workplace? How might being more real about your challenges inspire others to do the same?
- **In personal relationships**, consider where a deeper connection might be waiting on the other side of a difficult conversation. Like when my calls with my parents renewed our relationship, what relationships might be transformed if you had the courage to ask the questions you've been avoiding?
- **In your relationship with yourself**, ask what parts of your story you've been hiding—even from yourself. What might be possible if you finally acknowledged your full truth?

KEYS TO EMBRACING PROFESSIONAL VULNERABILITY

1. Practice Honest Reflection

Take time to reflect on the areas in your work and life where you feel guarded or disconnected. Ask yourself,

> What am I avoiding sharing or confronting?
> What fears or insecurities are holding me back from being my authentic self?

Write down your thoughts in a journal to gain clarity and start breaking down the internal walls you've built. Acknowledge your emotions without judgment and allow yourself the grace to grow.

2. Start Small and Share Intentionally

Vulnerability doesn't mean oversharing; it's about opening up in a way that builds trust and connection. Start with someone you trust—a trusted colleague, a coach, or a mentor—and share something you've been holding back, like a fear, failure, or challenge. This practice strengthens your ability to connect emotionally and shows others it's OK to do the same.

3. Set Healthy Boundaries

While vulnerability is powerful, it must be paired with clear boundaries. Identify what is appropriate to share in different spaces, like in your work life or business relationships. At work, be honest about challenges but avoid unnecessary oversharing. In business relationships, communicate your needs and expectations clearly. Boundaries ensure that vulnerability creates connection, not confusion or harm.

By reflecting honestly, sharing intentionally, and setting boundaries, you can begin to unlock the transformative power of vulnerability in your work life and business relationships.

KEYS TO EMBRACING PERSONAL VULNERABILITY

1. Reflect and Connect
Journal your thoughts. Take a few minutes each day to write down what you're feeling—your fears, your hopes, and things you're grateful for. This simple act helps you connect with your emotions and gain clarity.

Go for a walk with someone you love. Take a stroll with a family member, your partner, or your child. Use the time to share what's on your mind and invite them to do the same. Walks naturally encourage open, flowing conversations.

2. Nurture Relationships Through Simple Acts
Make a weekly phone call. Reach out to someone you love—a parent, sibling, friend, or mentor. Ask how they're doing, share something meaningful, and let the conversation bring you closer.

Write a letter. Sit down and write a heartfelt letter to someone you care about. Share your appreciation, memories, or hopes for your relationship. It's a deeply personal gesture that builds trust and connection.

3. Explore New Avenues of Vulnerability
Go on a journey of discovery. Take an adventure—a road trip, a hike, or even a visit to a new café. Use it as an opportunity to reflect on your own story and share pieces of it with someone you trust.

Try something outside your comfort zone. Join a group activity, take a class, or try a new hobby. These experiences often require a bit of vulnerability but can lead to unexpected connections and personal growth.

By integrating these small yet meaningful actions into your life, you'll begin to nurture vulnerability in both yourself and your relationships, creating deeper bonds and discovering new layers of authenticity.

CHAPTER FIVE
FORGIVENESS

Forgiveness is giving up the hope that the past could have been any different.

—Oprah Winfrey, *What Happened to You?*

I remember reading *The Lion and the Mouse* from Aesop's Fables when I was a kid. It was a simple story, but it stuck with me—how a mighty lion, capable of crushing a tiny mouse, chose mercy instead. And how, in an unexpected twist, the mouse later returned that mercy, gnawing through the ropes that trapped the lion, setting him free. What stuck with me even as a child was the idea that giving something to someone else can lead to the same thing being given to you. Mercy leads to mercy.

In the first chapters of this book, I've written about the ways the negative twin forces of anger and shame reverberated inside me, locking me in a dark loop of action and reaction that imprisoned me, body and soul. My redemption came by focusing on the powers at the other end of the spectrum, equally powerful but reverberating toward light and healing. Embracing them led to my own freedom. One of the most powerful of these forces is a close cousin to mercy, and that's forgiveness.

One of my favorite lines about forgiveness comes from another writer I read as a kid: Mark Twain. In *Pudd'nhead Wilson*, he writes, "Forgiveness is the fragrance that the violet sheds on the heel that has crushed it."

Like that crushed violet, forgiveness is not about seeking justice—it is about giving and receiving grace. It is what we offer not because the other person has earned it but because we refuse to let pain define us. It is the moment when the lion, instead of roaring in rage, lets the mouse go. It is the moment when the one who has been hurt chooses to unshackle their heart rather than live imprisoned by resentment.

I had to undo some knots to find my own way to forgive not just others but myself. As a kid, I'd constructed an emotional penitentiary around myself, forged from the raw materials of my traumatic past and the suffocating silence that draped over my family like a weighted blanket.

In my inner world, in my hood, and in my family, apologies were as rare as an Amur leopard. We had this skill of roller-skating over our conflicts without ever slowing down long enough to observe the damage caused. We'd step from heated arguments over past grievances to false reconciliations, never putting any genuine emotional sweat into it.

That lack of resolution had me deeply entrenched in layers of resentment, hurt, and anger, so fortified against the idea of truly pardoning myself or others that it once drove me to attempt suicide when I was sixteen, sitting in my basement bedroom with a loaded shotgun and bottle of pills. I had carried the weight of

CM attempting to molest me, being abused as a child, and feeling abandoned by my mother. That weight is what led me to that isolating moment in the basement. It wasn't just one singular bad thing I'd experienced; it was the cumulative weight of all the things bearing down on me at once.

On my own path, I have received forgiveness from a woman who had every reason to despise me: the woman who had told me she raised the man whose life I took. Yet instead of choosing hatred, she chose to release the weight of her pain—and in doing so, she freed both of us.

I had to find my own way to forgiveness—not just for others but for myself. I had to forgive the man who shot me, and I had to forgive my own mother for the wounds that ran deeper than the ones that bullets left behind.

Forgiveness is an affirmation of deep, radical, unconditional, and uncompromised self-love. It's now clear to me that being forgiven is a gift that we all have an opportunity to pay forward, and most importantly, forgiveness is one of the most liberating gifts we can give ourselves by receiving it when offered.

It's one thing to receive forgiveness from others and to forgive yourself. It's another to go there with someone else. That was still something I needed to learn.

In 2022, I got a phone call from Rick, a friend I'd made while inside. He had received a letter that was meant for me, written by a man serving a life sentence in prison. It wasn't uncommon for brothers on the inside to write and send letters to be passed on, so it wasn't a shocker that someone would send him a letter meant for me.

"It's from a brother named Terrence," Rick said. The name didn't ring a bell.

"What's it about?" I asked.

I heard Rick take a deep breath.

"You remember a woman named Tammy from Brightmo?"

"Sure, I know her," I said, not really getting where this was going.

"The letter is from her daughter's father. He's the guy who shot you."

Suddenly, I wasn't talking on the phone to Rick anymore—instead, I was standing on the corner of Blackstone Street, on the west side of Detroit. I was seventeen years old. There is the sound of gunfire, the smell of flesh burning—my flesh—and the feeling of blood gushing from my leg and foot.

The gun had been fired by Terrence. And thirty-two years later, he wrote to me.

"Send me the letter," I said, and then I hung up.

I sat back, staring at the phone on my desk. The universe was at it again. I had long ago pushed aside thoughts of ever putting a name to the shooter. That's when it hit me. My journey toward forgiveness was never meant to be a quick and seamless jaunt. It was a journey that would take me back to move me forward.

For thirty years Terrence was nameless and faceless—now the man who had tried to kill me had a name and a face.

He shot me on March 8, 1990—and Rick called me on that same day thirty years later. Was the universe trolling me? At first, I didn't even want to open the letter—this man had tried to kill me, and so much of what came after can be traced right back to that day. But here I was with Terrence's letter in my trembling hand.

For a fleeting moment, held deep within my body, I thought that with a few JPay messages and collect calls, I could have this motherfucker murdered for less than a thousand bucks. A prison yard is full of men who, for a fee, stood ready to do whatever someone asked—that's how some guys on the inside took care of themselves or helped their loved ones. The proverbial gun was in my hand, and it wouldn't take much for me to pull the trigger—he was completely vulnerable to my vengeance if I so wished; my influence still ran deep behind the walls.

I realized with a start that such fantasies could still exert a momentary chokehold on me. Briefly, the hot-headed seventeen-year-old still wanted revenge, to get my lick back. It was the way of the hood and prison yards I had grown up in, a code that says, "We can't be at peace until we get even."

But just as quickly I knew there was another option: I could choose to forgive this man and create a space of healing for both of us.

Too often my own trauma had led to me traumatizing others, but this brutal cycle could only be broken by someone taking action that didn't involve payback, who didn't believe in the possibility of "getting even." Life isn't even, isn't fair, isn't something that can be zeroed out like a bill.

Fortunately, by the time I got Terrence's letter, forgiveness and healing had become a much more important part of my inner math—I'd long since stopped thinking in terms of "even." Forgiveness was now an integral part of my healing and how I lived life. Almost twenty years earlier, I had received the astounding gift of forgiveness for the life I had taken. That singular act helped me embark on my transformative journey, one that compelled me to untangle the terrible choice I had made that night. This path of healing helped me recover my empathy and compassion—not just for that broken teenager I once was but also for others seeking my forgiveness. Others including Terrence.

I knew that forgiving him wouldn't be easy.

Like most people on their freedom journey, I was still figuring this shit out. It was a winding road, full of potholes, roadblocks, and obstructions around every corner, and here, now, was the mother of all potholes. But before I could let my trauma speak, I was reading Terrence's apology. His letter was powerful and profound. Through his words, this man came alive to me as a human being whose experience of trauma mirrored my own. I looked him up on the Michigan Department of Corrections website and studied his face before closing the computer and returning to his letter.

It was an extraordinary thing to read—this man who had caused so much suffering in my life was now taking ownership of it and apologizing in what I truly felt was a heartfelt way.

I'd carried anger and resentment toward him for so long, and reading his letter allowed me to begin to let go. I started to write back to him immediately, but I tore that letter up. And to this day,

I've yet to send him a reply. Some wounds are so deep as to be beyond words. What he did didn't just affect me—it affected my entire family deeply. And to be able to express that fully isn't in my writer's toolbox, not yet.

But while I have not yet found the words to send back to him, his own words released me to forgive him.

Instead of writing to him, I did end up finally writing to someone else I'd been avoiding.

As I've shared, my mother and I have always had a complicated relationship, made even more so by my time in prison and subsequent release. It took seventeen years for my mother to visit me in prison, and when I got out, it was challenging for us to connect.

For years, I resented her. I blamed her for my broken childhood and for the feelings of abandonment I experienced while in prison. But eventually I realized that I had to free myself from the idea that my mother or anyone else would magically morph into who I wanted them to be. Often our desire to forgive is motivated by the idea that the person we are forgiving will transform into our idea of who we think they should be rather than accepting them for who they are.

I wanted to really get to know my mother for who she is and forgive her without any expectations that she would become someone else. As part of that process, I invited her along on a trip with Liz, Liz's mother, Sekou, and me to an animal conservatory in Florida. It felt like the perfect setting to get to know my mother in a way that was far removed from our lived experience. For starters, the place was expansive and full of beautiful animals, many that were on the verge of extinction or endangered. This would be a safe place for us to get to know each other and learn each other's stories.

Through studying conflict resolution, I know that setting matters just as much as the individuals when it comes to fostering understanding and creating space for healing. In prison, resolving a conflict becomes significantly harder when everyone is watching, where it is all but impossible to pull someone aside for a private conversation. For this trip with my mother, I wanted a safe environment that didn't trigger one or both of us.

I have always loved animals. As a kid I was mesmerized by tapirs and kiwis, a flightless bird. My fourth-grade teacher, Ms. Papas, noticed my love of animals and gave me the great responsibility of taking care of our classroom pets: frogs, garter snakes, and baby chicks born in an incubator. She even let me take our garter snake home. Later, when I was a teenager living with my brother, I had two gerbils, two guinea pigs, a puppy, and a rabbit—it was a stressful time in my life, and this assortment of pets brought a sense of calm and purpose that distracted me from my damaging pursuits, things like selling and smoking crack while dodging and sending bullets in return.

It was an incredible trip. My mother shared with me the heartbreaking and traumatic things she experienced in her childhood and teenage years, and my heart burst open with a compassion that I had never experienced at that level. I shared things from my time in prison and my life after, and my mother wept in my arms. By taking time to understand her story, I was able to make sense of my own. We hugged tightly before we departed from Florida, her heading back to Detroit and me heading back to LA.

Still reflecting on that letter I'd received from the man who shot me, I found myself writing to her after the trip:

Dear Mama,

I have always dreamed of learning your story in your own words, through your eyes, heart, and spirit. I have dreamed of a moment in time when I could sit in your presence, feel your laughter from deep within, and witness you experiencing expanded joy. I have dreamed of watching you experience new things as you rediscover the boy now turned man who is your youngest son while holding your warm hands in mine. I have dreamed of the day when I could say "I love you, Mama" effortlessly and free of any attachments outside of the fact that you carried me and my siblings in your womb. I have dreamed of the day when we could sit in silence by a river, listening to the magic of nature swirling around us. I have dreamed of sharing the beauty of sunrises and the delightful taste of a perfectly baked oatmeal cookie. I have dreamed of listening to you tell me entertaining stories of your upbringing and discovering where my own ability to tell stories comes from. I have dreamed of the day when I can look in your face and see my own features reflected back. I have dreamed of the day when I can stand in front of you as a changed human, present father, and grown man and know that you see all of who I have become. I have dreamed of reaching the level of healing that allows me to be fully present in love and appreciation for whatever time we have left here on earth. I dreamed, I dreamed, I dreamed until my actions made dreams a reality.

Love,
Your baby boy, Shaka

Forgiveness is messy, often incomplete, and so difficult—and it doesn't have to be an absolute. If we think of forgiveness as a process, not a destination, then we will open the letter but maybe not reply to it; we'll write a letter and perhaps expect no answer, and that will be just fine.

What I took away from the experience with my mother is something I think you will find helpful on your journey. Be open to expressing your desires even though it may be extremely difficult and make you feel vulnerable. Let yourself try to forgive deeply while avoiding an expectation that a person will change because we forgive them. Let your forgiveness be forgiveness for you.

Receiving Terrence's letter and recognizing his humanity didn't absolve him of responsibility for the pain he caused, but it allowed me to let go of my anger and find peace within myself while finally putting a face to the ghost that for years had floated around in the background of my life.

Drilling Down

In my journey toward healing, I've discovered a series of affirmations and actions that have become my guiding light—steps toward reclaiming my peace and freedom.

First, I remind myself that I am inherently deserving of my own healing. There's no condition, no justification required for this truth—it simply is. Healing is not something I need to earn; it is my right as a human being.

I acknowledge that I am worthy of freedom from the pains that no longer exist in the physical realm but still linger in my spirit. These invisible wounds—memories of harm, moments of betrayal—may not be visible to the world, but they have left their mark. And yet I recognize that I have the power to release them, to stop carrying their weight.

I extend forgiveness to myself, knowing that it is never too late to grant myself the gift of self-love. I forgive myself for any delays, any moments when I didn't think I was ready to let go. I've come to understand that liberation doesn't adhere to a timeline—it arrives when I'm ready to receive it.

And today, in this very moment, I make a bold and radical choice: I forgive those who have harmed me. I do this not because I owe it to anyone, not because it's expected of me, but because I recognize that I deserve this gift. Forgiveness is not about them—it is about me. By releasing my grip on pain, I am claiming something invaluable: my freedom, my peace, and my future.

DIGGING DEEPER

Take a moment to reflect: Where in your life are you still carrying the weight of unforgiveness? What relationships, memories, or experiences have you been unable to release?

Consider how forgiveness might look in your own journey, not as a single event, but as a series of small choices that gradually lighten your load. What would be your first step? Who might you need to forgive—others or perhaps yourself?

Remember that forgiveness doesn't mean erasing the past or excusing harmful behavior. Instead, it's about choosing your own freedom over the continuing pain of holding on.

🔑 KEYS TO EMBRACING FORGIVENESS

1. Acknowledge the Depth of Your Feelings
- Don't just use angry language to describe your pain. Give your feelings specific, detailed language. When I reflected on the man who shot me, I dissected my emotions: I was afraid because I didn't know the shooter's face, but he knew mine. I was hurt because what I was shot over seemed trivial, yet I believed my life held more significance. I was sad because I felt betrayed, and I was angry because I couldn't seek revenge.
- Write out exactly how you felt and why. By laying out these feelings on paper, you break them into manageable pieces.

2. Visualize Life Without Negative Emotions
- Ask yourself, "How could this lead to being angrier, sadder, and more fearful?"
- Imagine being happier, more successful, and more fulfilled without these burdens. Visualizing this alternative can be a powerful motivator for forgiveness.

3. Meditate Daily on Your Desired Life
- Engage in daily meditation, focusing on the life you envision without the burden of anger, sadness, hurt, and revenge. This practice can help reinforce your commitment to forgiveness and your journey toward emotional freedom.

4. Practice Saying "I Forgive You"
- Verbalize your forgiveness. Speaking these words aloud allows the feeling to permeate your being in a profound way.

5. Acknowledge and Let Go of Resurfacing Emotions
- When old emotions try to sneak up on you, acknowledge them without allowing them to take root.
- Instead, reflect on your forgiveness mantra and commit to forgiving without attaching conditions to it.

6. Create Your Own Forgiveness Mantra
- Craft a personal forgiveness mantra that resonates with your journey. Repeating this mantra can help reinforce your commitment to forgiveness and emotional healing.
- I can't share mine because it's personal to me. However, you can create one that says something to this effect: "I forgive, and in equal measure, I recognize I am worthy of forgiveness."

7. Maintain a Forgiveness Journal
- Consider keeping a journal dedicated to forgiveness.
- Write down your thoughts, feelings, and reflections on your forgiveness journey. Documenting your progress can be a powerful tool for self-discovery and healing.

Remember that forgiveness is a transformative process that starts with acknowledging your worthiness. It's a journey toward emotional liberation and the path to experiencing the freedom of peace, joy, and prosperity in your life.

CHAPTER SIX
RESILIENCE

It doesn't matter if a million people tell you what you can't do, or if ten million tell you no. If you get one yes from God, that's all you need.

—Tyler Perry

I was on day three of fasting in solitary. I quietly declined each meal, even as my stomach clenched with hunger. For three days straight, I survived on nothing but tepid water from the sink and cherry cough drops from the commissary.

I had fasted before—for spiritual reasons, for discipline—but this time was different. This was not about faith. This was about survival. I was preparing my body for the possibility that the prison officers would one day decide to stop feeding me. I had assaulted one of their own, and I knew payback wasn't beyond them. If they wanted to punish me, they had options. They could starve me outright or, worse, put me on food restriction with the horrid concoction known as "food loaf," a hardened brick of everything from that day's menu mashed together into something barely fit for human consumption. I refused to be at their mercy.

The thought of what could come was terrifying, but in taking control of my own suffering, I found something unexpected: power. By voluntarily weakening my body, I was strengthening my mind. I was proving to myself that I could endure. I was vulnerable, but I was not powerless.

That's why I did it every month. Like clockwork, I would go three days without food, forcing my body to adjust, training my mind to push past hunger. Each time, I reminded myself, *If I can survive this by choice, I can survive it if it's forced upon me.* I was inoculating myself against fear—starving out my own anxiety before anyone else could use it against me.

It was only later that I realized I had unknowingly followed a lesson Lucius Annaeus Seneca wrote to his friend Lucilius in Letter 18 of his *Moral Letters to Lucilius*. Seneca, one of Rome's wealthiest and most powerful men, believed that true strength came not from luxury but from preparing for hardship. He urged Lucilius to regularly expose himself to discomfort to remind himself that he could survive without comfort: "Set aside now and then a number of days during which you will be content with the scantest and cheapest fare, with coarse and rough dress, saying to yourself the while: Is this the condition that I feared?"

Seneca's point was simple: He wanted Lucilius to understand that wealth and comfort were illusions of security. If we train ourselves to endure hardship, we free ourselves from the fear of losing it.

In that solitary cell, with nothing but hunger and time, I had unknowingly done the same. I had embraced weakness before it could be forced upon me. And in doing so, I had turned it into something else entirely: resilience.

In a culture that plasters the word "Grit" across T-shirts and coffee mugs, let me tell you—resilience is more than a catchy slogan or a motivational rallying cry for your sales team. Resilience is as much a spiritual principle as it is a psychological orientation. To get through the hard stuff, overcome obstacles, and truly break through, you must dig deep into the parts of yourself that others can't see. Like Winston Churchill may or may not have once said, "If you're going through hell, keep going."

Did it take grit to make it through my prison sentence, publish my first book, or create my first job? Absolutely. But that grit wasn't just surface-level determination. It was rooted in a hardcore belief I arrived at through sheer will and unrelenting resolve.

About a year into my prison sentence, I began to take exercise seriously. Before then, I'd stuck mostly to push-ups and sit-ups in my cell. But at Standish Maximum Security, I started to push myself further—I began doing pull-ups and trying my hand at distance running. When I first started, I could barely manage one or two pull-ups and could hardly run two laps around the track, which was only half a mile.

The first week was rough. Each day, I came out and saw almost no improvement. My body felt weak, and doubt crept into my mind. Why even try when it felt like I was going nowhere?

Then one day, I saw something that changed my perspective—not just on training but on life itself. It was during the Summer

Olympics in Barcelona, and the world was watching when Derek Redmond faced a moment of devastating pain. He was running the 400-meter semifinal when he tore his hamstring and collapsed on the track. Everyone thought his race was over. But instead of quitting, Derek stood up, limped forward, and kept going. The pain was written all over his face, but he refused to stop. And when his father ran onto the track to support him, the two of them crossed the finish line together.

I'll never forget that moment. It wasn't about winning—it was about finishing, about refusing to let failure define him. Derek's story reminded me of something Dieter F. Uchtdorf once said: "It is your reaction to adversity, not the adversity itself, that determines how your life's story will develop."

From that day forward, I approached training with a new mindset. It wasn't about where I started—it was about my willingness to keep going. I kept doing pull-ups until I could crank out sets with ease. I pushed myself to run farther each week, until I could complete laps without losing my breath. A year later, back at the Michigan Reformatory, where they had free weights, I started at the bottom again. My goal was to one day lift 225 pounds. It took years of consistent effort, but I eventually worked my way up, maxing out at 455 pounds and doing sets of fifteen with 225. I became one of the most respected trainers on the yard.

But what mattered most wasn't the physical strength I gained—it was the mental resilience I built along the way. And mental resilience turned out to be my path to freedom.

"What else can you do with your mind?"

Tom's question cut through the grunts of the weight lifters, the thud of the basketball bouncing on the carpeted court, and the stream of profanity echoing off the walls of the recreation center at the Michigan Reformatory—a place that was its own chaotic universe within the old walled prison. I'd been working for Tom as a recreation clerk for nearly a year, scheduling intramural sports events, ignoring the high-stakes gambling by the pool tables, and making sure the frequent fights didn't get out of hand. The rec center was the place where I operated my hustles, caught up with my homies, and stayed abreast of what was going on out on the yard. On Saturday mornings we ran pickup games for the best ballers on the compound, and during the week we ran baseball and football games between teams from the different cell blocks. It was one of the only jobs I had in prison that I enjoyed. I had access to everything, and working for Tom was like working for your cool uncle who let you get away with things your parents would never allow.

Tom wasn't like most of the staff. He wasn't interested in fights or gambling. He never preached or told us how to live our lives. Instead, he cracked jokes, talked to us about life on the outside, or asked us questions that made us think. His challenge—"What else can you do with your mind?"—wasn't just a casual inquiry; it was a turning point for me. It forced me to pause and reflect on my capabilities.

Tom one day told me he'd read an article I had written for the *Hill Top News*, our official prison newspaper. After jokingly quizzing me about whether I had written it or plagiarized it, he got serious and deep with me for the first of what would be many profound conversations. I told Tom that I had only written the article because a friend who worked at the paper asked me to write something after his main writer got transferred out.

"You're smart, Shaka. You're a natural leader. People will follow you—you just must figure out where you want to lead them," Tom told me. His words started me on a journey of self-discovery, writing, and, most importantly, resilience many years later. But this didn't happen overnight. It took five years after I left Tom at the Michigan Reformatory to find myself revisiting his question: "What else can you do with your mind?" There was power in that question. It acknowledged me as a person of worth and gave me something deep to ponder and eventually act on.

Six years later, sitting in solitary confinement, I began to dream of a life beyond the bars. I had been journaling and unearthing the past, but now I dared to dream of the future in an environment where most dreams are nightmares. I had a burning desire to write a book, but I didn't have a laptop, a typewriter, or even a proper pen. All I had was the vision and determination to do something meaningful with my mind. Completing a manuscript would be a symbolic expression that I could not only finish something tangible but also start the journey toward transforming my life. So I picked up my flimsy handmade ink pen, rolled it in paper, and started scribbling out my thoughts on whatever paper I could find. Each page led me one step closer to the new life I was creating.

As the saying goes, "You can't achieve what you can't conceive." I had heard those words many times. When I started to write my goals into existence, my fear and mental paralysis began to lift. When I shared my goals and dreams with the right people—those who challenged and supported me—they started to crystallize in my mind, which led to my action steps. It also gave those others permission to dream courageously.

In prison, books and writing were my escape and my education. I wrote every day and devoured philosophy and strategy, reading everything from Sun Tzu's *The Art of War* to Machiavelli's *The Prince*. The system was designed to limit how much we could become empowered: The wardens banned certain books and limited access to information. But I knew that to survive, I had to sharpen my mind, think critically, and stay ahead of anything I thought would hold me back, including my own dark thoughts.

I could feel the impact the books were having on me by how optimistic I started to feel inside. It was like the proverbial light at the end of the tunnel, except for me, each book was like a sliver of light inside the tunnel, guiding my steps. I could also see the impact of my reading showing up in the things I wrote in my journal. Philosophy was challenging me emotionally and intellectually in a way that I'd never experienced. For the first time in my life, I was asking myself tough questions: Will you push yourself when shit gets hard? How will you navigate this environment without resulting in violence? What are you willing to do to maximize your potential?

I was reading deep shit and loving it. I loved the Stoic philosophers like Marcus Aurelius, especially his *Meditations*. Up until then, I never thought about the mastery of emotions as a tool of power and personal agency. I loved the arguments of the Sophists because they reminded me of the verbal battles the men and I had in the law library. I even changed the names while reading Socrates's dialogues to make them more accessible. Instead of Glaucon, I used names like Tyrone, and instead of the cave allegory, I changed it to the basement allegory. Anything that challenged me to critically assess myself, remove all excuses, and master my mind drew me in.

I will never forget one day while reading this sentence from James Allen's *As a Man Thinketh*: "You will become as small as your controlling desire; as great as your dominant aspiration." I read it over and over before I was struck by the thought that I needed to write to the warden and try to convince him to let me out of solitary. If I was to get out of prison, I had to first get back to the general population. For many years, my controlling desire was to fight those who angered me, but in that moment, my dominant aspiration was to get out of solitary confinement so that, like they promise Army recruits, I could be all that I could be.

I wrote a letter to the warden—not just to ask if he would let me out of solitary but to declare my intention to live on my own new terms. The letter went something like this:

Dear Warden,

As you read this letter, I hope you will consider this essential question: What do you believe is true? When I first entered prison, I resolved never to follow the rules, to ignore any authority figure that contradicted my rebellious spirit. After nearly nine years in prison and thirty-five misconducts, it's evident that I have kept my word. So if you acknowledge my commitment to my word in a negative light, could you also believe in my sincerity about positive intentions?

If truth is what matters most in our dialogue, I encourage you to reflect on what I'm about to propose. Should you, on the off chance, allow me to reenter general population, I give you my word that for the remainder of my incarceration, I will dedicate myself solely to nurturing my writing talent and mentoring the young guys on the yard—gifts I discovered in this place and wish to share with prisoners and then the world.

Given your extensive experience in corrections, if you recognize that a person's word can be a testament to their character, regardless of past negativity, I hope you will give me a chance. Advocate for my release, and I promise to mentor other inmates upon my release, to publish the books I have written by hand, and to become an inspiration to many across the globe. It all hinges on one thing: your trust in my word.

Unexpectedly and surprisingly, I received a positive response from the warden. Writing that letter was how I ended up getting set free. I thought to myself, "This philosophical shit really works!" I had manifested myself back into the general population, even though it took some time for it to materialize. Thinking it and speaking it into existence were part of the process, but action and follow-through brought it all together.

Nothing came without adversity. After finishing my book, I got down on the floor of my cell and yelled under the door, "Does anyone want to read this book I just wrote?" Someone down the tier responded back, "Don't nobody want to read that shit. This ain't *Oprah*." For a second, I was taken aback and felt the old familiar anger surface: I could have this person stabbed when he got back to the yard. But instead, I did something better. I allowed his words to challenge me to think about exactly what I wanted from this writing thing, beyond having just anyone read it. I took his words and turned them into an audacious new goal: I wanted to write something worthy of Oprah Winfrey herself taking the time out to read it.

When I got out of prison after nineteen years, seven in solitary confinement, the world didn't exactly roll out the red carpet. I found myself standing in Rouge Park on the west side of Detroit, trying to sell my first self-published book. I felt out of place in oversized fresh-out-of-prison clothes and glasses that didn't quite fit. I'd expected the inside to be tough, but I didn't anticipate the cold shoulder from the streets. I remember one guy scoffing at me, saying, "People around here don't read."

But I didn't fold. I'd hustled in prison and on the streets—I wasn't about to let a little rejection stop me. I shot back with a smile, "Maybe not, but I'm sure someone you care about does. This would make a great gift, or at minimum you can place it under the leg of a wobbly table or couch." He laughed, and by the end of our conversation, I had $30 in my pocket.

That's when I realized I needed a strategy that included one of my strongest tools besides my pen: speaking. I started volunteering to speak at local schools, Job Corps, and anywhere else people would have me. Every time I spoke to an audience, I sold out all the books I brought with me. I wasn't just selling books; I was sharing a story, creating a connection, casting a vision. If I could get in front of people, I could make them see the value in my words.

One day, I received the list of attendees to a private event in Utah where I'd be speaking. I was floored—Mellody Hobson and George Lucas were going to be in the room. I knew I had to make an impression, and I decided that getting my book into the hands of the hundred participants was the way to do it.

But there was one problem: I didn't have much money. Between my business and personal accounts, there wasn't enough to comfortably cover the cost of giving away the hundred books, which came to $2,500. It was a big risk and a big pivot. After all, I was about to give away books to people who could clearly afford to pay for them. But I believed in my message, so I used nearly all the cash I had to print and ship the books to my friend Jess so they could be given out as I took the stage. When I finished my talk, I felt at peace. Even if nothing came of it, I knew I had left it all on the stage—I'd given it my all.

Later that day, a sharply dressed man approached me. He looked serious. I braced myself, expecting harsh words. But instead, he cracked a smile and said, "I'm upset with you." Before I could ask why, he continued, "My wife was in the room reading your book when we were supposed to be hanging out!" That man's wife, Andrea Wishom, soon became a dear friend.

After reading my book, without telling me, Andrea passed it along to Oprah. A year later—just five years after I'd gotten out of prison—I received a call that would change everything. Oprah wanted to interview me on *Super Soul Sunday*.

Months later, I flew to California for the filming. When I arrived at the hotel, I felt like a kid on the night before the first day of school. I laid out my clothes on the bed and even tried them on, sitting in a chair and imagining myself across from Oprah, preparing for one of the biggest moments of my life. I wore a light-blue polo sweater, a pair of nice jeans, Ferragamo loafers, and some cool socks. The next morning, I headed to her home, surprisingly calm—at least until the gates to the Promised Land (her estate) opened. That's when the old narratives started creeping in.

What if she brings up my crime and lays into me? What if she's afraid of me? What if she judges me?

As these thoughts raced through my mind, my nerves got the best of me, and I almost started shaking. But then I was stopped in my tracks by a simple, silly question: *What do you even call her—Ms. Winfrey? Mama O? Oprah?*

The thought made me laugh, and before I could come up with an answer, Oprah herself appeared. She called out my name in a singsong voice: "Shaka, Shaka, Shaka!" She wrapped me in a warm embrace, and in that moment, I knew I was safe. I knew my truth would be handled with care.

For the next three hours, Oprah guided me through my story. She drew out my truth with compassion, and we shared both laughter and tears.

When I returned home, I was on cloud nine. I was on my way to celebrate when I received a call—from Oprah. She said she wanted to make sure I had her personal number and told me, "I want us to be friends."

I couldn't believe it. Oprah—the most heralded and extraordinary woman in the world—wanted to be my friend.

From that moment on, we began exchanging texts and occasional calls. Yeah, I be texting Oprah.

Over the years, Oprah and I have worked on projects together, reached out to each other when the world felt like it was falling apart, and kept each other excited about the power of the written word. She has been an inspiration, a collaborator, and, most importantly, a true friend.

Every now and then, a small and petty part of me can't help but wonder out loud, "Where's that guy who told me this wasn't *Oprah*?"

The Business of Resilience

I carried that hustle—the grit, the determination, the resilience—with me into the business world. After leaving my role as executive director of ARC (Anti-Recidivism Coalition), I founded my own executive leadership and storytelling consultancy, Shaka Senghor Inc., and I found myself living my dream. Business was taking off. I had three six-figure contracts. And then the pandemic hit. In a matter of weeks, all the contracts were rescinded. Everything I'd built started to vanish.

In business, we throw around words like *grit* and *resilience* to inspire teams. But until you've stared down real adversity, you don't fully grasp what those words mean. I knew what it meant to be resilient because I'd lived it. The pandemic was just another challenge, another opportunity to adapt. That's what resilience is—finding new ways to succeed when the world tells you to stop.

In my case, when the pandemic gutted my new business, I shifted into the corporate world. Of course, corporations were facing their own reckoning: I joined TripActions, now known as Navan, whose travel business had been decimated almost overnight. But CEO Ariel Cohen never lost sight of the bigger opportunity. He told us that travel would return, and when it did, we'd be in the best position to serve the world. He was right.

Navan rebounded, and Ariel's leadership during that difficult time taught me that resilience in corporate America required the same focus, determination, and imagination required to get out and stay out of prison. It requires you to assess your situation honestly and learn from others who've faced adversity and come out on the other side.

Being part of a team with that mindset inspired me. It reminded me of what I'd done with my mind all those years before in prison—reshaping my thinking, educating myself, and building resilience through every setback. When I left Navan, I knew that whatever I built next would be even better because I had the confidence, the grit, and the resilience to make it happen.

Resilience in the Stories That Shaped Me

It's one thing to talk about resilience, but living it isn't always easy. Seeing past the setbacks requires you to dig deep. In my case, much of the fuel to keep going has come from the inspiration of others' stories.

Back in 2017 during a trip to Memphis, I visited the Stax Museum of American Soul Music to see Isaac Hayes's legendary gold-plated Cadillac Eldorado. I'd always been a Hayes fan—his music felt like soul food. But after watching a documentary on Stax Records, my admiration deepened. The label wasn't just a hit factory; it was a testament to entrepreneurial resilience.

Al Bell, who played a pivotal role in Stax's success, watched the label nearly crumble after losing its entire music catalog to a distribution deal with Atlantic Records, a failed partnership with CBS Records, and financial overextension. Imagine that—the legacy and the revenue stream destroyed. But instead of walking away, Bell doubled down. He rebuilt Stax from the ground up, gambling on new talent and fresh music. The result? A resurgence that produced some of the greatest soul music ever made. He later went on to produce hits like the rap group Tag Team's "Whoomp! (There It Is)" and Prince's "The Most Beautiful Girl in the World," proving that even massive setbacks are just temporary if you stay relentless.

That's the kind of resilience that inspired me during my darkest days inside. When you're isolated, with nothing but your thoughts and a few books, you have two choices: sink or rise. I chose to rise. I clung to the stories of those like Nelson Mandela, who spent twenty-seven years in prison but never lost sight of his greater mission. He once said, "The greatest glory in living lies not in never falling, but in rising every time we fall." That quote kept me alive in my toughest moments because I understood that resilience isn't about avoiding failure; it's about how you bounce back.

I dove into incredibly insightful books by brilliant and badass women, like Maya Angelou's *I Know Why the Caged Bird Sings* and Chin-Ning Chu's *Thick Face, Black Heart*. Chu wrote, "The ability to achieve your highest potential is directly related to your ability to battle through adversity, to develop an indestructible will, and to embrace the reality that success often demands a fearless heart and a thick face."

I read *The Autobiography of Malcolm X* and found the strength to redefine myself, to imagine a future where I was more than just another statistic. Malcolm showed me that no matter where you start, your story isn't set in stone. You have the power to rewrite it, but it takes grit and vision, and even when you waver, with enough belief in yourself, you can push through.

It wasn't just autobiographies that fueled me; other nonfiction and fiction writings played their part too. Books like Sidney Sheldon's *Master of the Game*, Stephen King's *The Stand*, and J. A. Rogers's *World's Great Men of Color* taught me that resilience shows up in the unlikeliest of characters—those who face insurmountable odds but still find a way to push through. Hannibal crossing the Alps on elephants wasn't just military brilliance; it was audacity. It's about believing that even when the road is blocked, there's another way through.

Life will invariably present us with opportunities to challenge our beliefs, grow stronger in our convictions, or buckle under the pressure. These choices, though uncomfortable, are the real gateways to our personal liberation. It is up to us, and us alone, to decide the direction we wish to take. Amid discomfort, chaos, and unsettling moments, I had a choice. It was one of my biggest life lessons—each moment we are in, we are always making a choice. Do we forge ahead in our minds or slink into that vacuous space that tells us we have no choice?

Every Setback Is a Setup for a Comeback

When I think about Al Bell rebuilding Stax, Nelson Mandela surviving twenty-seven years in prison, Maya Angelou writing over thirty books, Chin-Ning Chu teaching the power of resilience and strategic toughness, or Hannibal charging through the Alps, I'm reminded of what I've had to do in my own life.

When I was in prison, I didn't have access to technology, a publishing deal, or even the belief that people would care about what I had to say. But I wrote anyway. Later I hustled my books out of the trunk of my car, facing rejection after rejection, until finally, one ended up in Oprah's hands. That didn't happen because I had some master plan—it happened because I refused to stop. At that time there was no agent or publicist. All I had was pure grit, determination, the gift of serendipity, and the willingness to pivot instead of quitting when things weren't working.

Resilience is knowing that setbacks are setups for comebacks. It's that moment when you're at the end of your rope but find a way to tie a knot and hang on. It's taking that small, intentional step forward when the road seems blocked, trusting that persistence will lead to progress.

Resilience is about understanding that even when the world is stacked against you, the power to rise is within you. It's about looking for the Al Bells, the Mandelas, the Angelous, Chin-Ning Chus, and the Malcolm Xs and recognizing that their stories aren't so different from yours. They all faced moments where they could have folded, but they didn't. They endured, and because of that, they achieved greatness.

A Vision for the Future

When I look back at the path I've traveled—from scribbling notes in a prison cell to hustling books on the streets to stepping into the business world—I see a pattern. Every setback was an opportunity to grow. Every rejection fueled my next move. It's not about avoiding adversity; it's about embracing it, learning from it, and using it to propel you.

Resilience isn't a skill; it's a mindset that requires nurturing. You don't just get resilient, you go through shit, get stronger, go through more shit, get stronger, and when faced with more shit, realize your mind, body, and spirit working together is what it's about. It's the ability to take life's punches and keep moving forward and swinging back.

The Lesson Is in the Struggle

Resilience is in the struggle. It's in choosing to rise every time you fall. Whether it's overcoming the challenges of prison, navigating the cutthroat world of business, or facing personal hardships, the power to overcome lies within us. We just have to tap into it by acknowledging what we are going through, meditating on it, praying, and developing a working and practical plan of action that keeps us moving forward one thought at a time.

So ask yourself, "What else can I do with my mind?" The answer might just change your life.

Resilience is the process of bouncing back that you learn and relearn through life's inevitable challenges. It's not only something you're born with; it's something you build, moment by moment, choice by choice. Every setback I've faced has been an opportunity to dig deeper, to see what I'm really made of.

Watching Derek Redmond finish that race with his father's help taught me that resilience starts in the mind. It's not about avoiding pain or failure—it's about choosing to finish, no matter how broken you feel. That moment changed my perspective on what it means to keep going, even when the odds seem insurmountable.

Resilience isn't just about pushing through hardship. It's about recognizing that every adversity is a chance to grow stronger, both mentally and spiritually. Each time I found myself in a tough spot—whether it was the prison yard, solitary confinement, or the streets of Detroit—I learned that the key to getting through it wasn't running from the pain but leaning into it and learning from it.

At the heart of resilience is vision and determination. It's the ability to see a better future, even when your current reality seems bleak. Whether it was my goal to lift 225 pounds, write a book in solitary confinement, or get out and sell that book to people who doubted me, it was the clarity of my vision that gave me the strength to keep going.

But resilience isn't built in isolation. It's often the people who believe in us—like Derek Redmond's father—who help us get back up. I wouldn't have made it without mentors like Tom, who asked me what I could do with my mind, or Andrea, who passed my book to Oprah. Resilience is as much about building connections as it is about inner strength.

Most importantly, resilience isn't linear—it's circular. Every challenge builds on the last, teaching you how to navigate the next one. Each time I stumbled and got back up, I was training myself to see setbacks as setups for comebacks.

DIGGING DEEPER

How do you build resilience in your own life?

Begin by reflecting on your own resilience journey. Where in your life have you faced circumstances that seemed impossible to overcome? How did you respond when faced with rejection, failure, or seemingly insurmountable obstacles? What internal resources did you discover that you didn't know you had? What lessons did those experiences teach you about your own capacity to endure?

KEYS TO BUILDING RESILIENCE

1. Define Your Vision
- Think about one goal or challenge you're currently facing. Write it down in clear, actionable terms. Visualize your finish line and what success looks like for you.
- *Example:* If your goal is to start a new career, write down exactly where you want to be in five years, what steps you need to take, and why it matters to you.

2. Take One Small Step Every Day
- Break your goal into manageable pieces and commit to taking one small action each day, even if it's uncomfortable or hard. Progress, no matter how small, builds momentum.
- *Example:* If your goal is to get healthier, start with five minutes of exercise a day or swapping one unhealthy snack for something nutritious.

3. Learn from Your Setbacks
- Reflect on a time when you faced failure or rejection. Ask yourself, "What did I learn from that experience? How did it make me stronger?" Use those lessons to guide yourself forward.
- *Example:* Keep a journal where you document challenges and write about how you overcame them or what they taught you.

4. Build Your Support System
- Identify the people in your life who uplift and inspire you. Share your goals with them and ask for their support or guidance. Surround yourself with voices that encourage resilience.
- *Example:* Set up a regular check-in with a friend, mentor, or coach to hold yourself accountable and offer perspective.

5. Reframe Your Mindset
- Shift your focus from obstacles to opportunities. Instead of asking, "Why is this happening to me?" ask, "What can I learn from this? How can this make me stronger?"
- *Example:* Practice gratitude by writing down three things you're grateful for each day, even during tough times. Gratitude helps you see challenges in a more positive light.

Resilience isn't about being unbreakable; it's about finding the strength to put yourself back together, piece by piece, every time life tries to tear you down. It's about finishing your race, even if you have to limp across the finish line. These five keys to build resilience are tools to help you dig deep and build the kind of strength that carries you forward—not just for today but for a lifetime.

PART 3

EMBRACING FREEDOM

CHAPTER SEVEN
HOPE AND COMPOSURE

Hope smiles from the threshold of the year to come, whispering, "It will be happier."

—Lord Alfred Tennyson

I was about three years out of prison when I went out with some friends to celebrate. We decided to hit up a Detroit cabaret, one of those classic weekend events where promoters host a party, and the city shows up dressed to the nines. Cabarets are as Detroit as Coney dogs and Motown music—long-standing traditions where guests bring their own bottles of liquor, buy chicken wings and fries from the host, and dance the night away.

That night, it was summer, so the party had an all-white theme. The crowd was sharp—women in flowy dresses, men in linen suits, everyone looking like they had stepped off a runway. We were all just there to enjoy the night, but as we left the venue, the energy shifted.

A heated argument broke out between a young man and a security guard in the parking lot. Their voices rose, and the guard made a dangerous escalation: "I'm going to my car to get my gun." The threat was real, and suddenly, everyone was on edge. People started piling into their cars, some screeching out of the lot to avoid what might come next.

I had a choice: jump in my car and leave with the rest of the crowd or try to de-escalate the situation.

The stakes were high, higher than anything I'd faced while diffusing conflicts in prison. This wasn't just about calming someone down—there was a gun involved. But something inside me pushed me forward. I walked up to the young man, standing tall and rigid with anger, and met his gaze.

"Young brother, it's not worth it. Let's get you home to your family," I said, my voice steady and calm.

For a moment, I wasn't sure if my words would reach him. But then I saw his shoulders slump, the tension leaving his body like air from a balloon. Behind me, my friends Calvin and Jay worked to calm the security guard, who had made his way toward his car but was now hesitating.

After a long, tense pause, the young man said, "I'm going to listen to you, OG."

We helped him to his car, making sure he got in safely. Then, finally, I walked back to my own car, my legs heavy with the energy that had drained from me during those few intense moments. As I buckled myself in, I let out a long breath. *That was a close call*, I thought.

But that moment taught me two powerful lessons. First, in moments of intense conflict, sometimes all it takes is the hope of being seen and understood to shift the energy. And second, maintaining my own composure isn't just empowering for me—it's empowering for others. I don't recommend this call to action to anyone, but in that moment, it's what I was called to do.

As a kid, growing up watching *Mister Rogers' Neighborhood*, I learned about calmness and compassion as he thoughtfully and carefully discussed tough subjects. I never imagined those same lessons would play out in a parking lot in Detroit. But there I was, leaning on those childhood teachings. Mister Rogers showed me that calmness isn't passive—it's active. It's about meeting tension with presence, fear with understanding, and chaos with clarity.

In that parking lot, amid the shouting and threats, I wasn't just diffusing a conflict—I was honoring those lessons. Composure and hope don't just steady you; they steady those around you.

Hope was one of the tools I used to break out of my internal prison. It wasn't just a feeling or a vague wish—it was a force that kept me going when everything around me felt hopeless. Hope showed up in slivers of light, breaking through the cracks, reminding me that there was something worth fighting for on the other side. It wasn't about survival alone—it was about confronting the chains I couldn't see: the shame, fears, and anger I carried and the weight of narratives that told me my past defined me. Hope gave me the courage to believe those chains could be broken.

I found hope in unexpected places—in books that told stories of resilience, in fictional heroes who fell and rose again, and in the men working tirelessly in the prison law library to reclaim their freedom. I saw it in athletes who refused to quit, who kept getting up no matter how many times they were knocked down. I found it in music—my sanctuary—where lyrics and rhythms reminded me I wasn't alone. Those fragments of hope became lifelines, helping me imagine a life beyond my circumstances.

Hope rarely arrives all at once, but if you stay open to it, it will find you. It might come from a movie, a person, or even a song.

The Shawshank Redemption Is Illmatic

I finally saw *The Shawshank Redemption* after thirty years. It's funny how often people asked me about that film, assuming I'd seen it because of my time in prison. "Is that what it's really like?" they'd say, as if every prison experience can be summed up in a Hollywood script.

I was in prison when the movie was released. Prison banned movies and TV shows about incarceration, so while the world got to experience *Shawshank*, I was living my own version of it.

When I finally watched it decades later, one scene stuck with me like a memory I hadn't lived but knew in my bones—the conversation between Andy and Red about the power of music. Andy says, "That's the beauty of music. They can't take that away from you." He talks about how music offers a refuge, something untouchable, something that transcends the prison walls. And in a place where you're stripped down to nothing, that's everything.

Andy wasn't just talking about music. He was talking about hope, about composure, about the parts of us that no one can steal, no matter how much they try. "Hope is a good thing," Andy says. "Maybe the best of things, and no good thing ever dies."

It's wild to think that the same year *Shawshank* hit theaters, the greatest rap album of all time, *Illmatic*, landed in my life like a lifeline. I was at the Michigan Reformatory, three years deep into my sentence. The reformatory was a brutal place, a kind of gladiator school where survival wasn't just physical—it was mental. I remember that Nas's debut album had been given five mics in *The Source* magazine—an honor only bestowed on the best of the best. That was all I needed to know. I ordered the cassette immediately and waited.

When it arrived, I was ready. Sitting on my bunk, I pressed play and went on a lyrical journey with Nas from my prison cell all the way over to Queensbridge. Nas's adeptness at creating vivid images of inner-city life, coupled with profound poetic insights into the human experience, was a master class on what it means to be an artist. I'll never forget the moment "One Love" came on. It was like Nas was speaking directly to me, straight to my soul, when he spat, "What up, kid? I know shit is rough doin' your bid / When the cops came, you shoulda slid to my crib." I jumped off my bunk and started pacing the cell as the story unfolded. The raw and beautiful lyrics were a letter to a friend locked up, and at that moment, I felt like he was writing to me. I had felt abandoned, forgotten by so many people on the outside, from friends I hustled with to family members who treated me like a distant memory, but here was Nas, reminding me that he hadn't forgotten us. That album became my anchor. Just like

Andy's music, *Illmatic* was my refuge and a source of hope. So much so that I rushed up to the recreation center and went to the shoe room and got the worst tattoo ever for three dollars in prison tokens. I wanted to commemorate the album and its impact in a way that I would never forget. Instead of the elegant Old English or Garamond font, my tattoo was punctured into my skin in scraggly blobs of ink with a crude DIY tattoo gun made of a tape player motor and guitar string and ink made from unidentified ingredients. Along with the raggedy lettering, I added a dog biting through a chain to symbolize me breaking free. Instead of coming out like the Rottweiler image torn out of a magazine, it came out looking more like Fozzy the Bear.

Despite the butchered tattoo, *Illmatic* helped me find my composure. It reminded me that no matter how chaotic life was, no matter how much they tried to strip me down, I still had my mind, my spirit, my hope. And just like *Shawshank*, Nas's words reminded me that the world couldn't take that from me unless I let them.

Just over two decades later, through a series of serendipitous meetings, I was introduced to Ben Horowitz. At the time, Ben was preparing for an interview with Oprah at his company, a16z. During their conversation, he asked her a seemingly innocent question: *How do you get people to open up and cry during interviews?*

Oprah shared an anecdote and, in passing, mentioned the interview she and I had done on *Super Soul Sunday*. Intrigued, Ben later told his wife, Felicia, about the conversation and my story. Felicia, in turn, reached out to me via social media.

I'll never forget that first call with Felicia. She asked about my book, told me about Ben's meeting with Oprah, and then casually asked, "Are you familiar with my husband's writing?" I admitted I hadn't yet read his book, *The Hard Thing About Hard Things*, or his blogs, and she enthusiastically filled me in. Then she asked, "What are you into?"

"Reading and music," I said. "Mostly hip-hop."

"Who's your favorite artist?"

"Nas," I answered without hesitation.

"Wow. That's Ben's favorite as well."

Felicia and I wrapped up the conversation with some small talk before she extended an invitation: "Next time you're in the Bay, let's have dinner."

A few months later, I found myself in San Francisco. I reached out to Felicia, and she asked where I was staying. When I told her, she said, "I'm right down the street at Glide Church. Step outside, turn left."

At that moment, my curiosity kicked in. *Who are these people, and why are they so interested in me?* In hindsight, it made sense—my book was coming out, I was doing interviews—but at the time, I hadn't connected the dots.

I met Felicia at Glide, where she introduced me to Cecil Williams and Janice Mirikitani, who founded the church. Afterward, we parted ways, but later, she texted, "If you're free tonight, let's do dinner."

I agreed, and as I was heading over to the restaurant, Felicia texted again, "Actually, just come to the house." I switched the address in my app, and the driver remarked that we were going to Silicon Valley.

I'm going to be honest—when I first heard *Silicon Valley*, I imagined a valley full of titties. The only silicon I knew about was in fake breasts from the *Playboy* magazines I read in prison before they banned them. But as I drove through, the dark, tree-lined roads gave off a different kind of vibe. My *Detroit instinct* kicked in. *What if this was a setup?* I had seen *Misery*—I wasn't about to get hobbled out in the woods.

But once I arrived, my suspicions melted away. Their home was majestic, but more than that, they were *down to earth*. Ben was still on a call when I got in, so Felicia and I made small talk. When he finally joined us, Felicia immediately said, "He loves Nas."

Ben grinned. "Nas is a friend of mine."

I laughed, then told him the story behind my tattoo before pulling up my sleeve to show him. Ben nearly *fell out of his chair* laughing. My tattoo, faded and fuzzy, looked more like a bear than the image I had intended.

"I gotta call Nas," he said.

Right then and there, he dialed, and suddenly, I was talking to Nas himself, sharing my story. If it had ended there, I would have been satisfied. But it didn't.

Months later, Ben and Felicia invited me to a barbecue, mentioning that Nas would be there. When Nas arrived, we exchanged the universal Black man nod—a quick, understated *What's up?* Not long after, Ben invited me to a Nas and Lauryn Hill concert. The night was already surreal, but then Dave Chappelle walked up and asked if anyone had a cigarette. I didn't have any cigarettes, but I was happy to be talking to the legend himself. We laughed and traded jokes about him trying to find a cigarette before enjoying the concert.

That should have been enough. But it wasn't over.

One day, Ben hit me up again. "Come through—Nas is stopping by."

The three of us spent six hours together, just *talking shop*—hip-hop, culture, life. We were like teenagers, hyped up as we played song after song, dissecting every verse. Nas gave us backstories on albums and artists from the early days, and Ben and I shared our stories of the first time we heard different songs. It was apparent and refreshing that Nas was not only one of the greatest artists of all time; he was genuinely one of the biggest fans of the art form itself. Nas and I exchanged numbers before we departed and texted each other periodically about books we were reading or thinking of reading.

And then, years later, this happened: Sekou was away for a few days, and I was sitting home alone in my office during the pandemic when Nas reached out to me. He asked me if I could write something for a song he was working on for his upcoming album. Holy shit, the greatest lyricist was inviting me to contribute my words to a project. Nasir Jones, who had just won a Grammy for *King's Disease*, wanted me to contribute to *King's Disease II*. Imagine that—Nas, the same artist whose lyrics had carried me through my hardest days, now giving me the opportunity to do the same for someone else. I imagined my friends and other people serving time being shocked when they heard my voice come through the speakers. That was a moment where I had to draw on all the emotional strength I'd built over the years to keep my shit together. When Nas sent the text, I responded with a question: "When do you need it?" "I'm in the studio with the producer now," he replied. I would later learn that the producer was Hit-Boy, who also produced Travis Scott's "Sicko Mode," Big Sean's "Deep Reverence," and Nas's Grammy-winning album. Holy shit, I had to get straight to it. Fuck, I had to deliver, and I had to deliver now. I put my phone down and jumped out of my chair in my office. I was hyped up, and everything felt like a dream in slow motion.

Yo, the greatest lyricist of all time asked me to join him on a song. Nas had given me the song title and a simple direction, just freestyle but don't rap. I laughed out loud when I went back and read the text again. I gathered myself and began reciting the words into my voice memo right then and there—I didn't even take time to write the words down. I just spoke the words,

> Keep your composure
> On city blocks and cell blocks
> Keep your composure
> Hold it down, hold it tight
> Hold it close, hold space for yourself
> It's the way of the ancestors
> Our elders, our artists
> Our OGs, our dreamers, our builders

> With each breath, internalize their successes
> Their struggles, their sense of self
> Their sense of overcoming
> And take that power forward with you in life
> Remind yourself of the magnitude of your good fortune,

which are now a part of that Grammy-nominated album. Being a part of that album was a full-circle moment, a testament to the power of holding on to hope, to keeping your composure through the hardest times. It's proof that when you stay grounded, when you refuse to break, life can take you places you never dreamed of.

That lesson of composure, of holding steady, has played out in so many moments in my life. I think back to the time I went snorkeling in Maui. I'd never swum in the ocean before, and the waves were relentless. I was a good swimmer and even had a pool in my backyard, but this was different. Saltwater flooded my snorkel, and suddenly, I couldn't breathe. I couldn't put my feet on solid ground. The water was deep. Panic started to rise in my chest, and for a split second, I thought, *This is it*. But then I remembered something: Panic only makes things worse. So I took a breath and calmed myself. I removed the snorkel, started treading water, and swam back to the boat. It wasn't heroic, it wasn't grand—it was just composure.

Sometimes you just need to hold on until you get to the other side. It's not about pretending everything is fine or forcing yourself to feel strong—it's about finding the grit to endure, even when the weight feels unbearable and things beneath your feet feel unstable.

When Sherrod was murdered, I didn't have the luxury of falling apart right away. When our dog Indy was killed, I felt the same tight grip on my emotions and tears, holding myself together for the sake of my family. And when Sekou was diagnosed with type 1 diabetes, I had to hit the pause button on the fear, anger, and tears that burst from my eyes as I focused on the immediate task of being there for him, being his father and his buoy.

In those moments, I wasn't just holding on for myself—I was holding on for everyone who needed me. It wasn't about shutting down my emotions or pretending they didn't exist. Instead, it was about acknowledging them, letting them rest in the background, and focusing on the task at hand until I could find a moment to let it all go. Holding on meant becoming a grounding space for my family.

But composure doesn't make you superhuman. It's a delicate balance between strength and vulnerability. It's about understanding that the tears you hold back in the moment will eventually need a place to land. And when that moment comes—when you are in your car or at home alone, when everyone is safe or in bed, when the immediate crisis has passed, you allow yourself to break apart, to feel all the feels, and to begin healing. Holding on is an act of resilience, but letting go when the time is right is an act of self-preservation.

In those times, I had to be my family's rock and their safe space. I also had to break apart and put myself together in front of them. I had to give them hope, just like Nas's music gave me hope all those years ago. Composure meant showing my son that even though life had just thrown him a massive curveball, we could handle it together. And that is what composure really is. Sometimes you just need to hold on until you can safely and completely fall apart before putting yourself back together. It was twenty-seven years from *Illmatic* to *King's Disease II*, twenty-seven years between that moment of me sitting in that cell and me sending Nas the voice memo of my spoken word.

Composure isn't just for personal tragedy—it's also a critical tool in leadership, life, and business.

Composure isn't about ignoring challenges or pretending they don't exist. It's about confronting adversity head-on with clarity, focus, and a steady hand. Whether in life or in business, composure is the foundation that allows us to make thoughtful decisions, inspire confidence, and move forward, even in the most uncertain of times.

Like Andy Dufresne said in *Shawshank*, music, hope, and the things that can't be taken from us are what keep us grounded. Hip-hop has been my anchor, a source of strength and composure when the world around me was anything but stable. It's taught me to hold on to the things that are mine—my voice, my story, my hope.

Composure is also about embracing ambition unapologetically and allowing yourself to be driven by your passions and dreams. It's about recognizing the power of hope and using it to fuel your journey, no matter where you are or what challenges you face.

Composure as a Lifelong Practice

In the end, composure is not a destination but a lifelong practice. It's the art of balancing ambition with patience, of navigating the rip currents of life without losing your sense of self. It's about standing firm in your identity, even when others try to impose their narratives on you. And it's about knowing that, like the music that played in the background of our lives, there's something inside of us that no one can touch. It's ours, and it's enough.

The lessons I've learned from hip-hop, from the triumphs and setbacks, and from my own journey have all contributed to my understanding of composure. It's about staying true to who you are, holding on to hope, and pushing forward with unwavering determination while not losing your shit. And that, to me, is the ultimate expression of freedom.

Life has a way of testing us in ways we never expect. Whether it's the chaos of a parking lot in Detroit, the isolation of a prison cell, or the uncertainty of a rebranding effort in the corporate world, every challenge forces us to dig deep and find something steady to hold on to. For me, that steadiness has often come from two sources: hope and composure.

Hope is not just a fleeting feeling or a distant dream—it's a force that anchors us when the waves of life threaten to pull us under. It's the belief that even in the darkest moments, light can break through the cracks. And composure? Composure is the tool that helps us navigate those moments. It's not about shutting down or pretending everything is fine—it's about holding steady, even when the world around us feels like it's falling apart.

The lessons I've learned about hope and composure weren't just intellectual—they were forged in the fires of real life. From my time in prison, where hope was a lifeline, to moments in the outside world where composure helped me defuse conflict and lead with clarity, these lessons are deeply personal. And yet they are universal.

DIGGING DEEPER

Hope and composure represent the parts of us that remain ours, even in the most difficult circumstances—the internal resources that can't be taken away. So the question is, *How do you build these resources in your own life?*

Look for Hope in Small Moments
Hope rarely arrives in grand gestures—it comes in fragments: a kind word, a song, a book, or even a memory. Like when Nas's *Illmatic* brought me back to myself in prison, hope reminds us of what's still possible. What small slivers of light exist that you might be overlooking?

Hope Requires Action
Hope isn't passive—it's not just sitting around wishing for something better. It's about taking deliberate steps toward what you believe is possible. Identify a situation where you've been wishing instead of acting. What single step, no matter how small, could you take today to move toward what seems impossible?

Composure Steadies Those Around You
Composure is contagious; it creates space for others to feel safe and reconsider their choices. Think about a recent situation where someone else's lack of composure affected you. Now imagine a time when you maintained calm in the face of chaos. How did your composure affect others around you? Who might benefit from your steady presence? How could composure create space for others to feel safe and make better choices?

Composure Is a Lifelong Practice
Composure isn't something you master—it's something you practice every day. What small moment today might you use as practice ground? Perhaps it's a minor irritation in traffic, a challenging work call, or a difficult conversation. How could you approach this situation as deliberate practice rather than something to get through? What would staying steady look like in this specific instance?

KEYS TO BUILDING HOPE AND COMPOSURE

1. Anchor Yourself in Daily Rituals
- Hope and composure thrive on consistency. Create a daily ritual—whether it's journaling, meditating, or listening to music—that helps you stay grounded and connected to your purpose.
- *Example:* Take five minutes each morning to write down three things you're hopeful about or grateful for.

2. Pause Before Reacting
- In moments of tension or conflict, give yourself a beat to assess the situation before responding. This simple pause can shift your energy and prevent escalation.
- *Example:* When someone provokes you, take a deep breath, count to three, and ask yourself, "What's the best outcome here?"

3. Take Small, Consistent Steps Toward Your Vision
- Don't wait for everything to feel perfect before moving forward. Break your goals into small, manageable steps and commit to taking one each day, no matter how small.
- *Example:* If your goal is to write a book, commit to writing a hundred words daily, even if it's rough. Progress builds hope.

These keys and steps aren't just about surviving challenges—they're about thriving through them. By practicing hope and composure, you can create the space to face life's difficulties with courage and clarity, turning even the hardest moments into opportunities for growth.

CHAPTER EIGHT
LOVE

To love well is the task in all meaningful relationships, not just romantic bonds.

—bell hooks, *All About Love*

When news of our wedding made it into *People*, my phone started ringing off the hook. Friends from all over the world called, texted, and sent messages of love and congratulations. It was humbling to see our love story shared so publicly, but it also made me reflect on the journey that brought Liz and me to this moment. Marriage isn't just about the wedding day; it's about the love, work, and reflection that happen every day afterward.

As I thought about our journey, I was reminded of a modern parable I once came across on social media—the parable of the two mirrors. I'm unsure of the original author, but the story goes something like this:

A man and woman were given two mirrors on their wedding day. They were told, "These mirrors will show you the key to a happy marriage." Eager to unlock the wisdom, they looked into them—only to see their own reflections staring back.

Disappointed, the husband said, "This is just a normal mirror."

The elder who gifted them the mirrors laughed and explained, "Exactly. In marriage, you become a mirror to your partner. What you reflect is what you will receive in return. If you reflect love, patience, or understanding, you will get that back. But if you reflect anger, resentment, or indifference, that too will come back to you. A happy marriage is built not just on love but on the reflections you choose to create every day."

That story stuck with me because there are countless songs, scriptures, and pieces of wisdom reminding us of the importance of loving the person in the mirror. But marriage takes that lesson a step further: It asks us to reflect love even when we don't feel it, to choose grace over frustration, and to offer patience when it's needed most. Any married couple or long-term couple will attest that these things aren't easy, but they definitely are doable. However, they take a tremendous amount of effort—at least for me they do.

Antoine de Saint-Exupéry, the author of *The Little Prince*, once wrote, "Love does not consist in gazing at each other but in looking outward together in the same direction." That, to me, is what marriage is all about. It's not just about staring into each other's eyes in admiration; it's about building a shared vision—aligning our hopes, dreams, and efforts to create something greater than ourselves.

Every day with Liz reminds me that love is an active choice. It's a reflection, a direction, and ultimately, a journey we take together. But that is only one version of love.

Love like Liz and mine is often framed as romantic—a sweeping passion, a commitment to another person, a source of joy, and, sometimes, heartache. But love is so much more than that. It is the energetic force that connects us to others, the anchor that grounds us in our relationships with family and friends, and the force that fuels our passions and purpose. At its core, love is relational—it shapes how we interact with the world, how we give, and how we receive. Most importantly, love includes the relationship we have with ourselves. Self-love is the foundation of all other love. It's what enables us to show up authentically, to build meaningful connections, and to create a life that reflects our deepest values. Love, in all its forms, is the most powerful force we have—it heals, inspires, and transforms.

As much as I loved Liz, I knew it was important that I fully love myself. Like the other prisons I escaped, getting out of the prison of feeling unlovable for most of my life was a sacred and special journey that I am on to this day.

In December 2023, nine months before our wedding, I found myself at a crossroads. I had been navigating a period of profound grief, wrestling with my departure from a company I'd poured so much energy into and battling feelings of dissatisfaction with who I had become. To break this cycle, I decided to treat myself to what I anticipated would be a week of leisurely relaxation poolside—though, admittedly, I'd overlooked some crucial details in the fine print when booking my reservation. My destination: the Ranch Malibu.

The ride up the Pacific Coast Highway was nothing short of breathtaking. Waves crashed against the shore as swimmers and surfers dotted the expanse of beaches stretching from Santa Monica to Malibu. My car hugged the winding road, music thumping loudly, while the salty breeze flowed through my sunroof. The plan? Simple. Get my shit together. From the time I was released from prison, I had been on the go. I had worn myself down—working late nights, running on fumes, sacrificing sleep, and pushing my body past its limits. The weight crept up on me, the exhaustion became constant, but I kept moving, kept grinding. Like Mekhi Phifer's character Mitch said in the movie *Paid in Full*, "I love the game. I love the hustle." And I did. The hustle drove me, fueled me, made me feel unstoppable. But it wasn't just the hustle—it was the habits I had formed along the way. The lack of self-care, the missed doctors' appointments, the pain I ignored because I convinced myself I didn't have time to deal with it. Just like the prisons I've spoken about throughout this book, I was ensnared in the prison of grinding—believing that if I stopped, I'd lose everything I had built. In reality, though, I wasn't just grinding. I was being ground down.

As Anne Lamott put it, "Almost everything will work again if you unplug it for a few minutes, including you."

For the next seven days, I would hike, eat healthy, relax, and give up smoking the cheap cigars I had taken up fourteen or so years ago. Simple enough in theory, but I quickly realized this wasn't some casual wellness getaway—it was the real deal. By the time I arrived on a cool, rainy December day, I'd already smoked my last Black & Mild on the drive up, a small but symbolic step into the commitment I'd made to myself.

The place I had chosen wasn't just a retreat—it felt like a world unto itself. Nestled in the mountains with lush gardens, a spa, a heated pool, and an ice plunge, the setting was serene, almost cinematic. The private cottages were understated yet luxurious, with reclaimed wood floors, limestone bathrooms, and linen-covered beds that felt as inviting as they looked. The intimacy of the experience, with only a small group of participants, created a unique environment for deep, personal reflection and growth.

By the second day, doubt crept in. Did I really need to be here? Was this rest even necessary? The pull of the hustle, my home, and my habits gnawed at me. I told myself I was wasting time—that I had shit to do, deals to close, people to connect with. Slowing down felt unnatural, almost like failure. I had spent so long in motion that stillness felt like a prison of its own. A part of me wanted to pack it in, head right back down the coast toward my home. But I reminded myself that resistance was part of the journey toward self-love. Each time doubt surfaced, it was an opportunity to dig deeper, to confront the parts of myself that weren't ready to heal. Was this doubt I was feeling a kind of resistance—a battle between staying the same and allowing transformation to unfold? Why was I resisting a softer life and way of being? If I caved now, the possibilities waiting just beneath the surface would drown.

The week was a mix of grueling rain-drenched hikes, clean plant-based meals, daily massages, and quiet moments of introspection. The structure of the program pushed me in ways I hadn't been pushed since getting out of prison—physically, emotionally, and spiritually. By the final day, I felt lighter, clearer, more in tune with myself. My last hike was along the beach, the salty air filling my lungs as I reflected on the seven days of nourishing my body, mind, and spirit. I had done it. I had leaned into true self-love. As I packed my duffel bag and prepared to say my goodbyes to the people I had met, I was struck by a singular thought: For the first time in my adult life, I had treated my body with care, thoughtfulness, and nourishment for an entire week. I had eaten clean food and not put any impurities into my body. For most of my life, my norm was pain, discomfort, and pushing my body to the limits by eating crappy food and overindulging. Treating myself with care was a new and challenging experience. I felt a sense of pride that I had chosen myself for the first time in a long time.

But as I got closer to the city, the tug of the familiar pulled hard. Before I knew it, I had pulled over at a gas station and grabbed a pack of Black & Milds. Sitting in the car, I lit the first one, taking a long, deep inhale of disappointment. *What the fuck is wrong with me?* I thought. *Why can't I stay on a course that ensures my health?* The insistent cough I'd developed from smoking returned immediately. Damn! The seven days of work I had just poured into myself—all undone with a single puff. I felt myself spiraling.

And then it hit me: grace. I owed myself grace. When it comes to true self-love, grace is one of the main ingredients. Instead of sinking so far down that I couldn't pull myself back up, I decided to celebrate the fact that for seven days, I had fully loved myself. I made a vow to take it in chunks. For the next year, that's exactly what I would do—step by step, moment by moment. When I came up short, I wouldn't beat myself up. I'd just get back to it. I gave up the idea that everything had to be perfect. Perfection, I realized, had been a barrier to freeing my body. What was most important for me was taking the steps forward no matter how many missteps I had along the way. To me, focusing on progress over perfection is not only one of the greatest unlocks in love; it's also a key to unlocking the rest of life's gifts.

I remember one day talking with a friend about relationships, dating apps, and the whole circus of meeting people online. We laughed at the absurdity of it all—the horror stories and the brief glimmers of hope. But something she said stuck with me: "I just want someone who admires and respects me." I suddenly realized that admiration and respect were things I hadn't been prioritizing in my relationships. I had been focused on attraction, chemistry, and connection, but respect? Admiration? I hadn't put those at the forefront, not because I didn't value them, but because I hadn't fully understood how much they mattered.

That moment forced me to reflect, to step away from dating, from the casual hookups, and ask myself, "What does love look like when I truly love myself?" It was in this space of self-reflection that I started to understand what I was really looking for in a partner. I wasn't just looking for a romantic connection—I was searching for something deeper, someone who saw me, admired me, and respected me for who I was, and I had to offer the same in return.

I began to understand that love is about showing up in all the small moments, especially with my son, Sekou.

One story that stands out vividly in my memory is from 2016, during the NBA Finals. Ben called me up with courtside tickets to Game 7—the Cleveland Cavaliers versus the Golden State Warriors. LeBron James was about to make history, and I had the chance to witness it firsthand. It was the kind of opportunity you don't say no to. But there was one catch: It was Father's Day.

I had promised Sekou I'd be home to spend the day with him. He was only four and a half years old at the time, and he wouldn't have known the difference between Sunday and Monday. But in my mind, breaking that promise felt like a betrayal. I wrestled with the decision, torn between the once-in-a-lifetime experience and the commitment I'd made to my son. I was in LA and only a forty-five-minute flight and a Lyft ride away from the stadium.

Ultimately, I decided to fly home. We spent the day laughing, playing, and creating our own little memories. When Game 7 finally aired, I watched it at a local bar with friends. We had a great time, but a part of me was sick to my stomach that I had missed the opportunity to see LeBron, Kyrie, Steph, and Draymond in person at the same time.

The game itself was legendary. The Cavaliers, down 3–1 in the series, had battled back to force this decisive Game 7. No team in NBA Finals history had ever come back from such a deficit to win the championship, but LeBron James was determined to rewrite that narrative. From the bar, I watched the drama unfold while Sekou was at home in bed.

LeBron's chase-down block on Andre Iguodala, Kyrie Irving's clutch three-pointer, and the Cavaliers' nail-biting 93–89 victory became stories I could tell Sekou over and over as he grew older—as I reminded him of how much I sacrificed for him, like any good dad would do. LeBron's triple-double—twenty-seven points, eleven rebounds, and eleven assists—cemented his Finals MVP status and his legacy. But for me, the real story wasn't just about the game. It was about the choice I made that day to prioritize fatherhood over fandom.

The ambivalence pulled at me—not just in the moment but long after. Was the right thing to go to the game or be with Sekou? I told myself that showing up, being present, was what mattered most. But for whom? Him? Me? The guilt of choosing one over the other conflicted with my sense of duty. I had spent years as a father making decisions based on *good values*—responsibility, sacrifice, commitment. But what happens when those values come into conflict with *joy*, *authenticity*, or even *self-care*?

This, too, was a prison—even if a well-intentioned one. It's one of the hidden prisons we all face as parents, spouses, and leaders and in our struggle to love ourselves. The weight of expectation, of always doing the right thing, can keep us from doing the thing that makes us feel alive, fills us with joy, or allows us to take care of ourselves. We tell ourselves it's noble, that it's what's required, but sometimes it's just another way we trap ourselves—mistaking obligation for love, duty for purpose.

Sekou likely won't remember any details of that day, and I will always think back to that game and wonder what that experience was like in person. LeBron made history that night, but for me, it was a reminder that the most important choices and lessons happen off the court. And most of the time they come from the people we love.

In hindsight, I realize that decision came more from a place of guilt and fear than from love. I feared that if I didn't keep my word, I'd be failing as a father. The truth is, love isn't about making perfect decisions—it's about being present and showing up, even with all your imperfections. Sekou wouldn't have minded if I stayed an extra day, but I had placed an immense amount of pressure on myself to be the "perfect" dad in that moment, trying to live up to an ideal that didn't truly matter to him. It's a lesson I had to learn—love isn't about getting it right all the time. It's about being there, in whatever form that takes, and knowing that sometimes, love means letting yourself off the hook.

Love is complex and ever-changing. It's not something you "figure out" once and have all the answers—it's a continuous journey. Whether with your spouse or your children or even in your work, love demands patience, presence, and the grace to fail without fear. True strength in any relationship—personal or professional—comes from creating a safe space where growth, mistakes, and learning are not only allowed but embraced. Love isn't about perfection; it's about showing up, being present, and committing to the process.

My mother used to say, "Close the door! I'm not trying to heat the whole neighborhood!" when we'd leave the door open during Detroit winters. As a kid, I didn't fully understand that my mother was basically saying that you must keep something inside for yourself. But now I see it as a metaphor for being intentional about the love and energy we share—not just with others but with ourselves. If we leave the doors of our hearts and spirits wide open, without boundaries, we risk losing our warmth. Love requires that we conserve some of that warmth for ourselves so we can show up fully for others. As the saying goes, you can't pour from an empty cup. To truly love others, you must love yourself enough to protect your energy, to replenish your soul.

This lesson applies to more than just personal relationships—it's the same in business. When you show up in love—in love for your purpose, in love for the people you work with, and in love for the work itself—everything changes. Your colleagues, your customers, your team—they all feel that energy. Sure, you'll encounter curmudgeons and sourpusses along the way—people who run businesses on talent alone, without love—but the ultimate leaders, the ones who build something lasting, are those who lead with love or, at the very least, don't stand in the way of those who do.

Leading with love in business, in family, and in life doesn't mean being soft. Love has the power to transform every aspect of our lives, including the way we work. You can love your work, be passionate about your mission, and even care deeply for the people you collaborate with. That love can inspire you to lead with empathy, build trust, and create an environment where others feel seen and valued. But let's not confuse the love of work with the love we share with our family, friends, or even ourselves. Work, no matter how much we care about it, is still work. It requires boundaries to ensure it remains a part of your life, not the entirety of it.

We often see people invest so much emotional energy into their jobs that they lose sight of the distinction between professional commitment and personal connection. Fans get upset when athletes switch teams, and employees feel betrayed when colleagues leave for a competitor. But the truth is, loving the work doesn't mean staying in one place forever.

Sometimes, for your work or career to thrive, you need a new environment. Loving what you do doesn't mean sacrificing your growth or happiness—it means having the wisdom to make choices that align with your purpose. However, that wisdom doesn't come without pain. When it was time for me to leave Navan, I knew I would miss the people I worked alongside. We had built something special and had personal relationships. I would also miss going to the office, meeting new customers, and seeing the innovation in real time. Yet it was the right decision for me, and more importantly, it was the right decision for the company.

As a leader, love is one of the most powerful tools you can bring to the table. When you show up with love, you lead with compassion, build stronger relationships, and inspire others to do their best work. But love in leadership also means knowing when to step back, when to set healthy boundaries, and when to make tough decisions for the greater good. Boundaries are essential—not just for protecting your well-being but for preserving the integrity of your work and your relationships.

Love in the workplace is not about blurring lines—it's about showing up with authenticity, bringing your whole self to the table, and recognizing that work, while meaningful, is not the entirety of who you are. It's about creating a culture of trust and collaboration while keeping the balance that allows you to nurture other parts of your life. When you lead with love and maintain boundaries, you not only elevate the work itself—you create space for everyone involved to grow and thrive, including yourself.

It means being strong enough to show up authentically, to create spaces where people can thrive, and to make decisions from a place of respect and admiration. It means knowing that love is the foundation for everything else—whether you're on a Zoom call with your future spouse, keeping a promise to your son, or sitting courtside at the game of life.

Reflecting on these truths, I began to see patterns emerge—key lessons that not only shaped my relationship with Liz but also redefined how I approached love in all its forms. These lessons aren't confined to romantic relationships; they apply to friendships, family, and the relationship we have with ourselves. Here are the key lessons I've learned, along with actionable steps that can help us all deepen our capacity to give and receive love.

DIGGING DEEPER

For me, the journey toward understanding love began with the realization that I wasn't showing up fully for myself. After a series of failed relationships, I had to take a hard look at what love really meant—what it meant to love myself enough to open up to someone else fully. And that journey took time; I had to confront the gaps in my own heart.

Love Is a Reflection
In relationships, what you project—whether it's love, patience, understanding, or resentment—will often be reflected back to you. If you want kindness and love, reflect those qualities yourself. Healthy relationships are a mirror of our best intentions.

Love Is a Shared Vision
True love isn't just about emotional connection; it's about aligning your goals, values, and efforts to create something bigger than yourselves. Partners thrive when they look outward together and work toward a common purpose.

Self-Love Is Foundational
Self-love is the cornerstone of all other forms of love. Without it, we cannot show up fully in relationships, pursue our passions, or sustain meaningful connections. Loving yourself first creates the space to love others authentically.

KEYS TO LEADING WITH LOVE

1. Do This Daily Reflection Exercise

Take five minutes each evening to reflect on your interactions throughout the day. Ask yourself,

- What energy did I bring to my relationships today?
- Did I reflect the love, patience, and understanding I hope to receive?

If the answer is no, visualize how you'll adjust tomorrow. Over time, this practice creates mindfulness in your relationships and helps cultivate intentionality.

2. Create and Revisit a Shared Vision

Schedule a "vision talk" with your partner or loved one. Spend time discussing your goals, values, and dreams. Write them down and revisit them regularly. For example,

- Plan a monthly check-in to evaluate how you're working toward shared goals.
- Celebrate milestones together, no matter how small.

This exercise keeps both of you aligned and strengthens the bond through collaboration.

3. Practice Self-Love Consistently

Dedicate intentional time to nurture yourself mentally, emotionally, and physically. Examples include the following:

- *Morning affirmations.* Start the day by saying three things you love about yourself.
- *Self-care routine.* Choose one self-nurturing activity weekly, whether it's yoga, a long walk, or reading a book.

- *Forgiving yourself.* When you fall short, replace self-criticism with compassion. Remind yourself that progress, not perfection, is the goal.

Building self-love helps you show up as your best self in every relationship.

4. Celebrate Progress over Perfection
Keep a journal or notebook to track moments when you make progress in love—whether it's resolving a conflict calmly, setting boundaries, or showing extra patience. Celebrate these moments with a tangible action:

- Treat yourself to something small but meaningful, like a favorite coffee or time to relax.
- Share your wins with someone you trust, acknowledging the effort it takes to grow in love.

By shifting the focus to progress, you'll create a mindset that encourages persistence and resilience.

These aren't just lessons; they are keys to unlocking the deepest parts of yourself—your capacity to love, to reflect, to grow, and to show up fully in your relationships, parenting, and work. They guide you toward self-discovery, teaching you that love isn't just something you give but something you cultivate within, shaping every connection in your life romantically and professionally.

Love isn't about getting it right all the time. It's about showing up consistently, embracing the messiness of relationships, and granting yourself and others grace when things don't go as planned.

CHAPTER NINE
JOY

Let yourself be silently drawn by the strange pull of what you really love. It will not lead you astray.

—Rumi

Joy is a powerful force—it can pierce through even the darkest circumstances, offering light in places where it feels impossible to find any. Viktor Frankl wrote about this in *Man's Search for Meaning*, describing how, even in the unimaginable suffering of Nazi concentration camps, joy could be found in the smallest moments: a sunrise, a shared joke, or the memory of a loved one. For Frankl, joy was about not denying pain but finding something within to keep going.

I've experienced that truth firsthand. One day, a few months before I started working in the recreation center at the prison, I found Tom's wallet on the floor outside the office. It was stuffed with cash, his driver's license, and everything he needed to navigate his job in an environment where losing that ID could have gotten him suspended or even put the prison on lockdown. Without hesitation, I walked the wallet over to Tom and handed it back. His face lit up with gratitude as he thanked me repeatedly, but at the time, I didn't think much of it. I wasn't a thief, and returning it was simply the right thing to do.

What I didn't realize until later was how much joy Tom brought to that environment. He wasn't just the recreation supervisor—he was a lifeline. Tom greeted everyone with a smile, cracked jokes that could lift even the heaviest spirits, and made sure we had everything we needed to keep the sports programs running. He went above and beyond to create moments of levity and goodness in a place where those things were rare.

I'll never forget the first Christmas I worked for him. He brought in pizza and homemade cookies, a simple gesture that felt monumental in an environment like that. He even gave me a card to sign for my oldest son Jay and later slipped some money inside. Tom believed that joy wasn't just a luxury—it was a necessity. It wasn't until years later that I realized the depth of his lesson. Joy isn't something you wait for, it's something you choose to share, even in the hardest circumstances—like Frankl's sunrise or Joseph Campbell, who said, "Find a place inside where there's joy, and the joy will burn out the pain."

This call to look inward and Tom's kindness reminded me that even in the bleakest places, joy can burn away the pain.

For many years, I found myself locked in a tug-of-war between fully experiencing joy and tempering my feelings against the backdrop of my past. Coming out of prison, I carried a constant tension—a push and pull between gratitude for the life I now had and the guilt that came with having survived when so many hadn't. This tension wasn't just mental; it ran through me emotionally, spiritually, and physically. It's a weight many survivors of trauma, violence, and incarceration know too well.

One of the harshest realities of surviving trauma is the guilt that follows. It's not the kind of guilt that fades with time. It's deeper—more insidious. It's what Dr. William G. Niederland famously referred to as survivor's guilt in his work on Holocaust survivors—a feeling of undeserved survival, as though the fact that I was alive and free meant I owed something to those who weren't so lucky.

For years, I carried that weight like a lumberjack shouldering logs, dragging it through moments of triumph, through every celebration. It was hard to stand fully in my own light, haunted by the shadows of those I had left behind. It took me time to realize that the only way to experience joy fully was to accept that I deserved it, that I had a right to my own happiness and success. I had to turn my survivor's guilt into survivor's grace. This became apparent after my book *Writing My Wrongs* became a bestseller. I was invited to all kinds of experiences, from Oscar and Grammy parties to celebrity-filled dinners in my honor. But even still there was that constant nagging inside that didn't always allow me to be present in the joy of the experience.

In August 2023, Liz and I received an invitation to take a once-in-a-lifetime trip to Italy. The call was simple: "Get to Rome, and we'll take care of the rest." Over the weeks leading up to the trip, I caught glimpses of what was in store—luxury accommodations, a megayacht, a five-star chef, and stops along the Amalfi Coast and Pompeii. It sounded like a dream and a trip of a lifetime.

And yet as excited as I was, something kept me from embracing it fully. I felt disoriented, unable to plant both feet firmly in the moment.

Why couldn't I simply enjoy the trip? The answer, I realized, lay in the survivor's guilt I had carried for so long. I had survived the trauma of childhood, gun violence, and prison. I had made it out, while so many others hadn't. Every time I experienced something good—something joyous—I felt like I was betraying those who were still suffering. I had to remind myself that joy wasn't something I needed to justify. And that's what survivors often fail to realize. We tend to believe that the pain, guilt, and shame won't end and that love, joy, and success aren't meant for us.

This belief is often rooted in ego and in a scarcity mindset. Ego tells us that we are defined by our mistakes, our failures, and the worst moments of our lives. It clings to these narratives as if letting them go would strip us of our identity. Meanwhile, a scarcity mindset whispers that there isn't enough love or joy to go around: If you grab a bit, you're denying someone else. Others deserve it more, and you're unworthy. Together, ego and scarcity reinforce the walls of our internal prisons, convincing us that healing and abundance are out of reach. Yet the truth is, abundance flows when we release the need to hold on to what no longer serves us and allow ourselves to embrace the possibilities beyond our pain.

I meditated to liberate myself from that nagging feeling and leaned into the trip. And what a trip it was! Every moment, every conversation, every meal, every day, there was magic, love, revelation, and more joy than I ever knew existed. I chose joy, and joy chose me. We rode jet skis, vibed out in the hot tub on the back of the yacht, bounced from island to island, shopped in Capri, and even witnessed a volcano erupting. If I had let that voice from the past take over, I would have missed out on the chance to experience the highest level of joy possible.

Eckhart Tolle's *The Power of Now* became the inspiration for a mantra I used to support this shift: "You have the power right now to decide your experience. You have the power to accept this incredible gift. And you have the power to enjoy the shit out of it without feeling guilty for it!"

It's about living fully in the "right now" moments. When I embraced that, everything began to shift. I understood that joy didn't erase my past, but it allowed me to live beyond it. Experiencing joy meant I could finally live the life I had envisioned for myself and my family, free from the chains of my history.

I have to admit I still struggle with learning how to embrace joy, whether in the grand, picture-perfect moments or in the cracks, in the everyday. But now I find that watering my plants or watching my wife and son light up with excitement brings me joy. I realized that joy is a practice—something you nurture, like a garden.

One day, while scrolling through Instagram, looking for a recipe, I stumbled upon a viral video of a teacher and her students performing Michael Jackson's "Thriller" music video choreography in perfect sync. There was something so pure about it—the joy on their faces, the way they moved together, free and uninhibited. I craved to have that kind of experience of unbridled joy. That freedom to just be. Witnessing joy like that always stirs something deep inside me. It reminds me of how much I had denied myself those feelings, how much I had distanced myself from experiencing life's fullness.

Growing up in a tough environment, where masculinity was equated with stoicism and toughness, created barriers I didn't even realize were there. I was taught not to feel, not to cry, not to emote—not because of philosophy but because of survival. In a world shaped by trauma, gun violence, and PTSD, emotions were a liability, and vulnerability could get you hurt. It was an extreme form of stoicism, not the kind preached in boardrooms or self-help books, but the kind that kept you alive. We weren't mastering our emotions to build resilience in business—we were shutting them down to avoid becoming a target. Social norms told me that vulnerability was weakness, that showing joy or softness made me less of a man. These unspoken rules conditioned me to suppress emotions, to see happiness as fleeting or undeserved. Over time, I built walls so high around my heart that even when joy knocked, I couldn't let it in. But moments like the ones that played out in the video—when joy is undeniable—remind me that breaking down those barriers is where true freedom begins.

A few years after I was released from prison, I was invited to Big Bear Lake, California, to speak at an event called Unique Camp, hosted by a woman named Sonja who is now a dear friend. My two younger sisters, Nakia and Shamica, along with my friend Calvin, flew from Detroit to LA to join me. The following day, we piled onto a bus with a lively group of campers and wound our way up the mountains to Big Bear Lake.

What I encountered over the next few days was far removed from the streets I had come home to and the prison I had left behind. People danced like no one was watching, laughed freely, and radiated an effortless peace. They smiled as if unburdened by the weight of the world. Even my sisters, who weren't exactly known for stepping outside their comfort zones, were celebrated for diving into the activities, making new friends, and dancing on tables like they had been born for it. Watching them embrace the moment was beautiful, but it also stirred something in me. I realized how much I wanted that joy for myself but had never allowed it. I had become so accustomed to denying myself happiness that even witnessing it in others felt foreign.

Over time, I began leaning in. One night, I climbed a hill and marveled at the stars, amazed at how close the moon seemed up there in the mountains. The last morning, I even agreed to join the group for the polar bear plunge. As I got ready to leave my cabin, stripped down to just a towel, my roommate stopped me in my tracks, laughing hysterically. I had misunderstood the concept of the plunge and thought it meant going in completely naked. Embarrassed but amused, I hurried back to grab some shorts before joining everyone at the pool. The plunge was freezing, but it left me invigorated, alive, and, most importantly, laughing with a group of people who had embraced me as one of their own.

That weekend in Big Bear Lake wasn't just a trip; it was a turning point. It was the first time I allowed myself to feel the fullness of life again—to let joy, laughter, and connection break through the walls I had built. It reminded me that the barriers I thought were protecting me were actually keeping me from the things I needed most. Joy, as I learned that weekend, isn't something you wait for; it's something you step into, even if it feels unfamiliar at first.

I also began to understand something important: I'd often avoided joy out of fear. Afraid that if I let myself feel it, it would be taken away. But the truth is, by avoiding joy, I'd missed much deeper connections—deep love, the freedom to dance, and the ability to just be myself in relationships. I had to drop my guard, learn to be vulnerable in conversations and in moments of pure celebration without shrinking in shame or guilt.

These days, you might find me wandering through used bookstores, hunting for first-edition treasures, or unlocking the forgotten boxes of life's little joys like driving with my music blasting and saying yes to more adventure. I'm breaking free from the ruts of the day-to-day; leaning into the simple, unfiltered joy of children; and reintroducing play into my life—not as something scheduled or structured but as an organic way to rediscover happiness. Play isn't another job on the to-do list; it's a state of being.

I wouldn't call myself an enthusiast just yet, but I'm getting there. Whether it's spinning records, hiking with my family, or working out with my son, I'm finding more ways to embrace joy. It's not about perfection; it's about presence. And with each small moment, I'm learning to savor life just a little more.

Healing, I've learned, isn't a one-time event. It's not a moment of clarity that suddenly fixes everything. My soul was battered for decades, and healing those wounds didn't come from a few therapy sessions or reading a self-help book. It took years of digging deep and clawing my way back to the surface. My spirit was torn apart by a fractured home, the griminess of the streets, and incarceration. My body was torn apart by bullets, beatings, and bars. My heart was torn apart by the loss of my brother and our puppy. And I've had to work to stitch the pieces of myself back together over and over again. Finding or reclaiming joy was integral to that stitching.

There are days when I still feel the weight of past trauma trying to insert itself into my current life. On most days, I can find joy in the things I truly love, like great music, time spent with family, or a good book. But on other days, the past pokes at me, reminding me of where I've been.

Living in joy has required me to be present in the fullest way possible, to acknowledge that I am worthy of all the good life has to offer. Today, I find joy more easily because I look for it in the everyday. But it's not just me; people all over are searching for joy and meaning. Sometimes it's getting away from a brutal news cycle, breaking away from doom scrolling, or just enjoying life. The more I search for joy, the more things I discover along the way.

DIGGING DEEPER

For much of my life, joy seemed like a fleeting sensation—tied to moments of success, immediate gratification, or the temporary highs of accomplishment. But as I delved deeper into my personal journey, I realized that true joy required me to go beyond the surface. It wasn't just about what felt good in the moment but about how my choices resonated holistically with my values, my long-term vision, and the life I wanted to build.

As a writer and speaker, I knew my work would impact others. I understood that my words and stories could inspire change, spark conversations, and help people transform their lives. But I also knew that passion alone wouldn't sustain me—or my family—financially. While mentoring and advocating for others brought me immense fulfillment, it also came with moments of heaviness, where the emotional toll felt almost unbearable. I had to figure out how to navigate this dynamic—how to sustain my work without depleting myself.

Through this process, I realized that joy is more than just fleeting moments of fun; it is the result of aligning passion with purpose. It's what I now call moving from fun to fulfillment. It's about finding joy in my purpose and allowing that joy to sustain me, even when life feels heavy.

But this isn't just about me. The question is, Where do *you* find joy? Maybe you're already leaning into it, or maybe you're still searching for that connection. Either way, it's worth asking yourself,

- Does your work bring you joy?
- Are you passionate about it?
- Does it align with your values and long-term vision?
- Can you sustain yourself and the life you want while doing it?

If the answers aren't clear, that's OK. What matters is taking the time to reflect and allowing yourself to discover joy—not just the fleeting kind but the kind that fills your life with purpose and meaning.

🔑 KEYS TO CULTIVATING JOY

1. Discover Your Ikigai

Ikigai, a concept that originated in Okinawa, Japan, is loosely translated as "a reason for being." It dates back to the Heian period (794–1185 CE) and has been a guiding principle in Japanese culture for centuries. The idea of Ikigai encourages individuals to find the intersection of four elements. When they align, you discover your Ikigai—a life of purpose and fulfillment.

1. What you love (your passion)
2. What you're good at (your skills)
3. What the world needs (your mission)
4. What you can be paid for (your profession)

Write down your answers to these four questions, consider them, and see how they line up with your current life. Consider what changes you could make to find greater purpose and fulfillment in your own life.

2. Become a Joy Hunter

Actively seek out joy in your life, not as a passive by-product but as something you cultivate intentionally. Here are some steps to guide you:

1. *Remember the last time you leaned into a joyful moment.* When was the last time you felt pure joy? What were you doing and who were you with? Use that as a starting point to create more of those experiences.
2. *Make joy part of your budget.* Whether it's financial, emotional, or time-based, invest in joy like you would any other necessity. Treat yourself to a hobby, plan a trip, or set aside time for something you love.

3. *Reconnect with childhood joy.* What did you love to do as a kid? Buy a coloring book, do a puzzle, play a game, or go outside and explore. Let yourself be playful and curious.
4. *Find other joy hunters.* Surround yourself with people who value joy and encourage you to pursue it. Whether it's through a hiking group, a creative class, or a weekly meetup, joy is amplified when shared.
5. *Do something new or unexpected.* Challenge yourself to step outside your routine. Try a new recipe, take a pottery class, or spend an afternoon exploring your local area with fresh eyes.
6. *Spend time in nature.* Go for a hike, take a walk, or sit outside and soak in the beauty around you.

Choosing joy isn't just about feeling good—it's about living fully. It's about aligning your passions and purpose, fostering deep connections, and creating a life that feels vibrant and meaningful. When you embrace joy, you don't just live—you thrive.

So ask yourself, "What's in it for me when I choose joy?" The answer is simple: "Everything." Joy fuels you, connects you, and makes life worth living. And when you start seeking it intentionally, you'll discover that the journey of being a joy hunter is just as fulfilling as the joy itself.

CHAPTER TEN
SUCCESS

I attribute my success to this: I never gave or took any excuse.

—Florence Nightingale

We often look at the lives of people we believe have "made it" without realizing that what we're seeing is the finished product. The polished success story often hides the countless hours of effort, sacrifice, and learning it took to get there. What I've come to understand through observation and conversations with people who have been successful in business, sports, marriage, and life is this: Success is always a process.

For some, it meant staying late at the office or gym, waking up an hour earlier, reading that extra book, seeking out a mentor or coach, and consistently going above and beyond what was required or expected. When I connect the dots across those conversations and analyze the outcomes, my friend Ben's words resonate deeply: "Success is about making one smart decision after another, and most of those decisions depend on the mindset you bring to the table."

But Ben also reminded me of an equally important truth: Failure works the same way. It's often the result of one poor decision after another. He asked me questions that forced me to reflect on my own failures:

Did you overlook something you should have noticed?
Did you ignore key details that might have changed the outcome?
Did you fail to care enough to follow through?

What I realized is that failure isn't a single catastrophic event. More often, it's the result of small missteps that compound over time. But those missteps, while painful, are also the greatest teachers. Every failure contains lessons about what to do differently, where to pay closer attention, and how to adapt.

Recently, I saw a video of a lion sitting under a tree. It looked as though the lion had sought out the tree for shade from the relentless sun. While it sat there, something unbelievable happened—an impala fell from the tree, almost like manna from the sky. The lion stared at the impala in what seemed like utter disbelief, as if it couldn't comprehend its luck. And why would it? Lions don't sit under trees waiting for food to drop from the sky. In their nature, lions hunt—they stalk, they chase, they work for their meals.

It's the same with success. Yes, every now and then, someone will get the luckiest break and have their version of an impala fall from the sky. But for the rest of us, like a lion living in nature, we have to go out and hunt for success. We have to take deliberate steps, fail, learn, and try again—because success isn't an accident, and it certainly isn't guaranteed.

What I've learned is that the road to success and the road to failure often look remarkably similar at first. Success is built on a foundation of small, intentional actions taken consistently over time. It requires attention to detail, persistence, and a willingness to learn from every setback. Failure, on the other hand, often stems from neglecting those same principles.

When I think about the stories of those I admire most, they all follow this universal truth: Success is earned. It's not about luck or waiting for your opportunity to fall into your lap—it's about staying committed to the process.

So when you think about the freedom of success, I encourage you to ask yourself, "Am I taking one smart step after the next, or am I sitting under the tree, waiting for success to fall into my lap?"

The ownership of success lies in your choices, your actions, and your willingness to go out and hunt for it. To reach success, you have to own it! And remember, even if you stumble or fail, each misstep is just another opportunity to learn, grow, and get closer to your goal.

The Inner Battle

Success, to me, has always been a battle fought on the inside. It's a relentless duel between the voices of my past—those broken, cynical echoes—and my authentic voice that knows I can harness the power of the universe for good, including my own greater good. I realized early on while journaling in solitary that the key to success was in feeding the right voice, starving the wrong one. This is the essence of mentally "writing my wrongs."

The negative voice doesn't just disappear; it lurks in the background, waiting for a chance to surface. It's there every time you say you're triggered, reminding you of its presence. But by acknowledging it, I've learned to control it.

Writing My Way Out: The Power of Words

When I first heard the song "I Wrote My Way Out" by Nas, Lin-Manuel Miranda, Aloe Blacc, and Dave East from the play *Hamilton*, it felt like the universe was speaking directly to me. Indeed, I had written my way out of prison and up into a position where I could help others. My escape wasn't just from the physical confines of incarceration; it was a mental and emotional liberation through the power of ink and paper.

For years I journaled and made notes in the books and articles I had read from authors who had overcome the odds, escaped their own hidden prisons, and found success despite the odds they had faced.

I crafted a new escape plan—one built on three pillars: ideation, activation, and manifestation. I spent hours imagining my new life, down to the smallest details, like the car I would drive and the family dynamics I desired. Next came activation, taking immediate steps to turn my dreams into reality. Finally, through consistent action, I manifested the life I had envisioned. Step by step, I was getting my *SHIT* together.

Own Your SHIT: A Blueprint for Success

Owning my SHIT has been a guiding principle for my success. It's a reminder to take full responsibility for my journey, broken down as follows:

- *Success.* Only I can define what success looks like for me, whether as a partner, employee, or entrepreneur. While others can contribute to my success, it's ultimately my responsibility to chart the course.
- *Hustle.* The drive to pursue my ambitions comes from within. Yes, others can inspire or push me, but I am the one who must get up and go after my goals.
- *Intelligence.* I am the architect of my mind, responsible for feeding it the knowledge and skills needed to succeed. Recommendations from others are valuable, but it's up to me to apply them.
- *Talent.* We all have innate talents, but without practice and dedication, they go to waste. Honoring my gifts means continually challenging myself to grow.

Redefining Success

Joining Navan in 2020 was a transformative step in my career. My journey with Navan took me from being a consultant to being in the C suite. I found myself working alongside sales leaders, learning and growing with each step, misstep, success, and failure. One of the most surreal moments was being invited to the New York Stock Exchange as the VP of corporate communications. Standing on that historic floor, I was reminded of the incredible distance I'd traveled—from the mean streets of Detroit and solitary confinement to the heights of corporate America. Navan's commitment to creating a people-first workplace—the importance we placed on workplace experience, from food, to pets, to fun, to encouraging our employees to travel and experience the world—resonated deeply with me. The environment was encouraging and inspiring even when it was tough, and I was proud to represent a company that truly valued success not just as a business metric but as a human experience.

Not every project was a success. I took on roles that weren't the right fit, shouldered more responsibility than was wise, and often failed to ask the right questions up front. There was no logical reason for me to leave my role as head of sales and success culture. I loved that job. I thrived in it—training our staff to become incredible storytellers, helping young reps and account executives sharpen their craft. They were true hustlers, and there was nothing more exhilarating than hustling alongside go-getters.

But I got caught up in the allure of growth. The VP of corporate communications role seemed like an opportunity to step outside my comfort zone, to stretch myself in new ways. I didn't ask the right questions. If I had, I would have realized that the thrill of pitching our product at South by Southwest, hosting tech execs at company parties, and scoring front-row tickets to music venues would be replaced with drafting customer emails every time a travel crisis hit. Had I known, there's no way I would have taken that role. I would rather have watched paint dry.

Reflecting on that experience taught me the importance of pausing, assessing, and ensuring that the roles and projects I took on were truly aligned with my skills and values. I promised myself that I would never take on a job title or agree to work on a project that snuffed out my imagination.

After launching the rebrand at Navan in my role as VP of corporate communications, I knew it was time for me to move on from corporate America as an employee and focus on my creativity and the investment opportunities that had come as a result of my work in Silicon Valley over the years. It was a risky leap, but I felt prepared for it.

Master Your Thinking, Master Your Destiny

Success isn't an end point; it's a continuous journey that requires mastery over one's own thoughts and actions. It's about taking the tools of survival and transforming them into instruments of success. It's about the hard-earned lessons, the unique experience of going through hardship and thriving in spite of it while using what you know to get you where you are trying to go. It's about rejecting excuses and fully embracing the responsibility for your own path.

What helped me was that I had a greater fear of stagnation than of failure. It felt scarier to remain in place than to step into the unknown and move toward my larger goals. So stop emptying your tank for everyone else and start fueling your own journey.

Reflecting on my journey—from being imprisoned to becoming a *New York Times* bestselling author, a TED speaker, and an MIT Media Lab fellow and being featured in documentaries like Emmy Award–winning *13th* directed by Ava DuVernay—I realize that success didn't come in a straight line. It wasn't about one big win—it was about consistently showing up, day after day, with discipline, focus, and an unwavering belief in my own potential. It was about being creative and wild with my imagination and pushing past the boundaries society set for me. It was also about having the guts to walk away when things no longer served me or simply for a new adventure.

That belief was fueled by stories of others who had dared to dream big, like Richard Williams, the father of Venus and Serena Williams. He saw greatness in his daughters long before the world did, and his belief, combined with their relentless discipline, incredible talent, and sheer determination, changed the world of tennis. Or Tom Brady, the underdog drafted 199th overall who went on to become a seven-time Super Bowl champion. These examples remind me that success is built on more than talent—it's about foresight, discipline, and an unshakable commitment to your vision.

People often focus on the end result—on the shiny surface of success. But success is built in the grind. It's in the extra hours spent refining your craft, in the late-night brainstorms, in the resilience you build when things don't go as planned. Success is a practice—it's not a one-time achievement or an end goal. It's the willingness to keep going when things get tough, to adapt and adjust your course when challenges arise, and to believe that the best is still ahead of you. Success is about staying open to the possibilities, recognizing that there is so much more to experience and explore.

The accomplishments I'm most proud of weren't the result of luck or even pure talent. I've been in dark places—feeling hopeless, lost, depressed, and angry. There were moments when the weight of my circumstances felt insurmountable, when the path forward seemed invisible and the darkness seemed to stretch endlessly. But success wasn't about some magical turning point or an overnight transformation. It was built slowly, steadily—brick by brick.

One of the most transformative lessons I've embraced is the value of doing the hard things first. Facing the difficult conversations, tackling the challenges I wanted to avoid, and embracing discomfort head-on. I had to have hard conversations with myself when I left my executive director position at the ARC and again when I left my role at Navan. Did I have enough money to get by while I got clients, booked speaking engagements, and worked on deals to pay me? Did I have the support I needed to make such a bold leap? Was my decision going to have a negative impact on Liz and Sekou's quality of life? I had to curb my spending, balance my budget differently, and contract my lifestyle where needed. I had to invest my money in things that may or may not return anything and turn down guaranteed money when it didn't align with my vision. It wasn't easy—it required grit, courage, and belief in the possibility of something better. But the more I leaned into the hard things, the lighter life became. Each obstacle I overcame added strength to my spirit and clarity to my vision.

When people look at my life or the lives of others, they often see the highlight reels but miss all of the seconds, minutes, and hours of hard work and the many years of doubt and instability. Being featured on Nas's Grammy-nominated album wasn't just a moment of serendipity—it was the culmination of years of building relationships, of honing my voice as a writer, and of having the courage to step into spaces where I wasn't always comfortable.

Success is layered. It's not just financial or professional—it's emotional, mental, and spiritual. It's about alignment, about creating a life that not only supports your dreams but elevates the people around you. That's the lesson I've learned: Success isn't about titles or accolades; it's about living in harmony with your purpose and making sure that every step you take is a step toward your highest potential.

The journey isn't over. Every day is an opportunity to grow, to build, to redefine what success looks like. It's about continuously betting on yourself, pivoting when necessary, and never losing sight of the vision that set you on this path in the first place. I'm evolving and looking to go on the next adventure and look forward to meeting you along the way.

DIGGING DEEPER

Reflect on your own relationship with success by considering these insights:

Success Is a Process, Not an Event

Success isn't something that happens overnight. It's built through consistent, small actions; discipline; and learning from failure. What small and consistent actions are you taking that might not feel significant right now but are building toward something meaningful? Where might you be overlooking the process while waiting for "the big moment"?

Failure Is a Teacher, Not a Life Sentence

Every failure carries valuable lessons—overlooked details, ignored warnings, or lack of follow-through. Think about your most recent setback or disappointment. What specific lessons did it contain? How did you course correct?

You Have to Hunt for Success

Just like a lion doesn't wait for food to fall from the sky, opportunities won't simply appear. In what areas of your life are you passively waiting for opportunities instead of actively creating them? Consider a goal you've had for some time. How might your progress accelerate if you approached it with determination and active pursuit?

Master Your Mindset, Master Your Life

What internal dialogue plays on repeat in your mind when you face challenges? Which voice is louder: the one that believes in your potential or the one that reminds you of past failures? What daily practice could help you strengthen the voice of belief?

Success Requires Strategic Growth, Not Just Any Opportunity

Not every promotion, title, or project is aligned with your purpose. The wrong move—no matter how prestigious—can take you away from your passion. Look at your current commitments and opportunities. Which ones truly align with your vision and values? What would it mean to release something that looks successful from the outside but doesn't fuel your inner purpose?

KEYS TO FINDING SUCCESS

1. Audit Your Daily Choices
- At the end of each day, ask, Did my actions move me toward success or failure today?
- Identify one small adjustment that can improve your trajectory tomorrow.

2. Develop a Failure Analysis Practice
- Instead of fearing failure, study it. After a setback, ask,
  - What did I overlook?
  - What could I have done differently?
  - What lesson can I apply moving forward?
- Write these reflections down to recognize patterns and make better decisions.

3. Create a "Hunter's Plan" for Your Goals
- Define one big goal and break it into actionable steps.
- Schedule one bold action each week (e.g., pitch an idea, reach out to a mentor, invest time into a new skill).
- Track progress and adjust as needed—success isn't linear.

4. Rewrite Your Inner Narrative
- Identify one limiting belief you tell yourself (e.g., "I'm not ready" or "I don't deserve this").
- Replace it with a new affirmation (e.g., "I am prepared to grow" or "I create my own opportunities").
- Reinforce this mindset by journaling, meditating, or speaking it aloud daily.

5. Vet Every Opportunity Before Saying Yes
- Before accepting a new role, project, or challenge, ask,
  - Does this align with my vision?
  - Does this fuel my creativity and growth?
  - What am I giving up to say yes to this?
- If the answer doesn't support your long-term vision, walk away with confidence.

CHAPTER ELEVEN
FACING DOWN FEAR

Remembering that you are going to die is the best way I know to avoid the trap of thinking you have something to lose.

—Steve Jobs

The Relic and the Hustler

Fear could have been the force that kept me from pursuing my dreams of becoming a bestselling writer. I had every excuse: I was too old, the era of hustling books from the trunk was over, the street lit phenomenon had faded. But I chose to say, "Fuck it. I'll give it a go." I knew that while I might look outdated or out of touch, I could turn those perceptions into advantages. I was a relic from the past, but like all great relics, I believed I held real value.

Having spent two decades trapped in a prison time capsule, I embraced my out-of-place look—oversized shorts and baggy T-shirts. People laughed, but they also reached for their wallets.

I had a powerful story to tell, one that spanned trauma, solitary confinement, and the many atrocities of my young life. And I was delivering it with a smile. I was present, and my presence spoke volumes.

I knew how to sell. I'd been selling since I was thirteen years old, from drugs on the streets to hustling whatever I could on the prison yard. Deep down, I was a hustler's hustler, and I knew that other hustlers would see and respect that. They were seeing an OG who had turned his life around. What they didn't know was that inside this OG was a genius, one who had rediscovered himself through some of the toughest times imaginable. My appearance was a testament to my journey, and I was here to share it with the world. It was my time to go.

Facing Fear in Rouge Park

I invited family and friends to join me on a book-selling excursion to Rouge Park on Detroit's west side. Their overwhelming response was "Hell no." One friend even warned, "Niggas get shot up there all the time." Despite this, I felt drawn to that place. I wasn't afraid; I felt inspired and compelled, believing that my audience lived there—the people from the hood who understood my story.

I stepped out of my little Honda Civic into the world I knew so well. Hood cars rolled by with big, shiny rims; music booming from trunks; and scantily clad women dancing to the beat. I felt the stares of men tracing my steps, but these were my people.

This was my home, and I knew my story would resonate here if it would resonate anywhere.

Years later, I would find myself in a similar battle with fear, but on a much bigger stage. In 2014, I received an invitation from June Cohen, head of media for TED, to speak at their thirtieth anniversary, which was going to be held in Vancouver, Canada. This wasn't just any platform—it was *the* stage. TED was a global arena where thinkers, innovators, and dreamers shared ideas that they hoped could change the world or at least the conversation. I had been given the opportunity to share my truth about incarceration, redemption, and second chances. But as soon as I accepted the offer, a new fear emerged: my felony record.

Canada was going to bar my entry due to my criminal history. After all the work I'd done, after all the progress I'd made personally and professionally, I couldn't escape a terrible decision I made decades ago. The weight of that reality hit hard. But then, June and I came up with a plan: I'd give my talk via livestream from their New York office.

The day before my talk, I felt the familiar hum of nerves. What if I mess up? What if I freeze in front of the camera? What if I fail?

To calm my nerves that night, I headed down to the hotel bar and ended up in a beer-drinking contest with a couple of strangers. I drank myself into a fog, trying to escape the mounting anxiety. The next morning, it felt like a sack of cement had been dropped on my head and a pair of Timberland boots was tumbling around in my stomach. Michael, the speaking coach assigned to me by TED, asked to meet over at the office for a "dress rehearsal." I was confused—I had never heard of this term, and I couldn't quite understand why they wanted me to rehearse how I dressed. I had been putting my clothes on just fine since I was a kid! I called a friend of mine and asked about this. He burst into laughter and explained to me what it meant. I was learning.

I headed over to the office, and they miked me up for a test run via the live stream. On the other side of the screen, Chris Anderson told me to deliver my talk looking at the camera. As I responded that I wasn't done memorizing the talk yet, I could feel those Timberland boots kicking harder. I could hear my heart beating in my head. Chris told me to just freestyle it so they could make sure everything worked. I stumbled through a half-hearted attempt to remember the talk, and they said everything was working and to come back in a bit after I finished memorizing it.

I went into a room off to the side and tried to remember the talk, but every time I put the paper down, my mind went blank. I was panicking, but then I remembered the advice I had given to a friend who was prepping for his own TEDx Talk a couple of years earlier: Just tell your story. So instead of worrying about the script, I decided to speak from my heart.

When they were ready for my run-through, I pointed to the camera crew, making them my audience, and I let my story flow out of me, raw and real. But just a few minutes in, static filled my earpiece, a technical issue the crew caught relatively quickly. All seemed ready to go.

When it was time to go live, I stood in the middle of the room and started: "Twenty-three years ago . . ." Before I got to the next line, the earpiece filled with static again. I couldn't hear myself, and I didn't know if anyone on the other end could hear me either. "What if they don't catch it in time?" I thought to myself. Sweat started to roll down my back, and my hands dampened. For the briefest second, my feet felt like cinder blocks as panic rose in my chest. In that moment I could have stopped and signaled to the audio/visual team that something was wrong, but I made a choice to keep going.

Whether the audio was working or not, I was going to deliver my message, and I did. When my twelve minutes were over, I had no idea how it had landed in Vancouver. I couldn't see the faces or hear the reaction from the people on the other side of the camera. Instead there was the camera crew and a small group of people who were invited to the TED office in front of me. But then my phone buzzed with a text from my friend Baratunde: "Bro, I just watched your talk here at the conference. They gave you a standing ovation." He later texted me the reaction, which I watched throughout the night as I celebrated with a small group of friends.

That moment taught me that fear only topples you if you give in to its power. I had learned how to push through. I had learned how to use the fear as fuel.

Fear has shown up many times in my career. But here's the thing: It is a part of the journey. Don't pretend it's not there. Acknowledge it, embrace it, and then move forward anyway. Every time I've faced and gone past fear, I've found that the other side holds something far more powerful: freedom.

At the end of the day, fear is only as strong as the story you tell yourself about it.

Confronting the Inner Voice

The most important conversations we have are often the ones with ourselves, yet they are also the most fearsome. Engaging in these dialogues without censorship, filters, or limitations liberated me. The hardest conversation I had was confronting the voice within—my self-accusing spirit cloaked in shame and humiliation. When I left Navan, I was pretty beat up from everything that had transpired over the years. In addition to the deaths of Sherrod and Indy and Sekou's diagnosis, I caught COVID four times, developed cluster headaches, and had back-to-back dental surgery. Life was beating me down in a way I hadn't experienced in a long time, which brought up familiar feelings of uncertainty and instability. I was afraid but knew I had to push on; otherwise, I would have been stuck in neutral.

The Prison of Fear

Fear is a prison we often build ourselves, a fortress constructed from ignorance, antipathy, and the desire to control perceived threats. It paralyzes us, silences us, and keeps us from pursuing the life we want. We fear what people will think, we fear losing love, we fear judgment.

Fear doesn't need to control us. It's a voice that can be subdued and managed. It's about recognizing that fear is always present but that we have the power to confront it. For me, naming my fears, understanding their origins, and choosing to face them instead of running away was the path to freedom.

Anxiety has been my lifelong companion, manifesting in various ways—worrying about being on time, finding parking, dealing with other people's emotions. It's easier to handle these things alone than to carry them into interactions with others. Yet surviving and overcoming these anxieties and recognizing the survivor's guilt that comes from succeeding when others do not have been profound parts of my journey.

There's an actual name for an intense fear of failure: atychiphobia. And of all the things I fear, the most intense for much of my life was a fear of public speaking. Ever since I was a kid, I dreaded exposing my gap teeth and my big head. Yet I found a way to conquer that fear by redirecting that inner energy outwardly. Doing the thing I feared most, with literal static threatening to drag me down, led not only to a standing ovation (which I didn't even get to see) but to knowing I'm strong enough to handle it. I still get nerves—who doesn't?—but they don't hold me back.

DIGGING DEEPER

I had to ask myself, "Who am I if I don't accomplish everything on my vision board? If success—by society's standards—never comes, then what?" The fear of failure loomed large, but I came to understand that my worth isn't defined by accolades, titles, or wealth. My worth comes from within.

Yes, I still wanted to achieve the goals I had set, earn the money I desired, and travel the world. But at my core, my deepest desire was simpler—to live a life of creativity in a way that allowed me to care for my family and stay true to my soul's calling.

So I ask you, How does this way of thinking impact the quality of your life? Are you fully present with yourself, or are you chasing a version of success that was never truly yours? Are you trusting your divine calling, your inner guide, or are you lost in expectations that don't align with your spirit?

These questions aren't just for me. They're yours to carry, to reflect on, and to answer in a way that leads you closer to your truth.

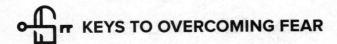 **KEYS TO OVERCOMING FEAR**

---

1. Acknowledge Fear Without Surrendering to It
Recognize fear's presence in your life without letting it dictate your choices or limit your potential.

2. Reframe Your Narrative
Transform fear's power by changing the stories you tell yourself about what scares you and what those fears mean.

3. Use Fear as Fuel
Convert the nervous energy of fear into motivation that propels you toward your goals rather than away from them.

4. Redefine Success on Your Own Terms
Liberation comes when you measure achievement by internal fulfillment rather than external validation or societal expectations.

CHAPTER TWELVE
BECOMING UNSTOPPABLE

The question isn't who is going to let me; it's who is going to stop me.

—Ayn Rand

When I think of fearlessness, I think of being unstoppable. And the one image that continually comes to mind is Diana Ross during her iconic Central Park performance. Born in Detroit, Ross wasn't just a singer—she was and is a force of nature. On that unforgettable day in Central Park, the skies opened up with a raging storm that threatened to stop the show. Yet Diana Ross stayed on stage, hair and dress blowing in the wind, drenched but undeterred, delivering one of the most powerful performances of her career. She didn't just sing—she commanded the environment, bending the elements to her will. Watching that performance over and over, I related to the way she remained graceful and regal amid the relentless chaos. It reminded me that even in the face of adversity, we have the power to make the world serve us if we refuse to yield.

That image of Ross, drenched and unstoppable, stayed with me as I forged my own path. After leaving Navan, I was at another crossroads. I had invested three years of my life into the company, pouring not just time but money into its success. Even when I knew it was time to move on, fear crept in. I had survived tougher times, no doubt, but this was different. When you're at the bottom, the stakes are actually pretty low. It's different when you're responsible not just for yourself but also for your family.

I had to figure out what was next, but instead of letting fear consume me, I went back to the baseline that had carried me through my darkest moments—the belief that I was capable of more, that I was destined for greatness.

I didn't waste time. I had the honor of being a fellow at the Virginia Tech Institute for Leadership in Technology, a prestigious one-year program that integrates the humanities into leadership through courses in philosophy, religion, arts, and history. My speaking engagements increased, and I invested in new ventures. I started moderating high-level conversations, like those at the Paid in Full Foundation event, where I interviewed hip-hop luminaries Rakim, Scarface, and Steve Stoute, and the Green Carpet Fashion Awards, where I worked with Chris Bevans and introduced John Legend for his award. My success wasn't just about achieving milestones—it was about constantly growing and evolving. Being successful and unstoppable meant believing in my own magic and having a healthy ego. And it also meant pushing forward, regardless of how loud the inner doubts got. I have previously spoken of ego in a negative sense—egotism, arrogance, the need for validation—but there is another side to it, one that deserves nurturing and belief. A strong, healthy ego isn't about self-importance; it's about self-trust. It's the foundation of confidence, the force that allows us to stand firm in our decisions and take bold action. Sigmund Freud recognized this when he said, "The ego represents what we call reason and sanity, in contrast to the id which contains the passions."

In other words, ego—when balanced—grounds us. It keeps fear in check, tempers impulsive desires, and allows us to move forward with an unstoppable spirit. Believing in yourself is not just a lofty ideal; it's a daily practice, especially when you're locked in a constant battle between your best and worst thoughts. On the toughest days, I leaned into self-talk, reminding myself of my worth and potential. I revisited old journals where I had poured out dreams, challenges, and victories, rediscovering my resilience in the process. I immersed myself in books that inspired me, filling my mind with wisdom and encouragement. Podcasts on entrepreneurship and leadership became a daily ritual, providing insights and stories that reignited my sense of purpose.

I didn't do it alone either—I reached out to my network of friends for motivation and inspiration. Their encouragement reminded me of the power of community and the importance of surrounding myself with people who believed in me. Music also played a significant role. I listened to aspirational hip-hop that spoke directly to my soul, weaving hope and determination into every verse. I went down the proverbial rabbit hole with artists like LaRussell, Black Milk, and Boldy James along with the standards that defined my era.

The one thing I refused to do was get stuck in a loop of negativity. The moment a negative thought surfaced, I countered it with positive affirmations. I meditated on gratitude, grounding myself in the blessings I already had rather than the challenges I faced. This commitment to shifting my mindset wasn't just about pushing through—it was about creating a foundation of self-belief that allowed me to see possibilities instead of obstacles and to keep moving forward with hope and purpose.

It's easy to get caught up in fear, to let it keep you stagnant. Once you're in your fifties, culture tells you to stop—you're done being interesting. But there's so much proof of people my age who found success in their later years. Ray Kroc didn't start on his path to turn a small burger stand into the global McDonald's empire until he was fifty-two. Toni Morrison published *The Bluest Eye* at forty, later becoming a Nobel Prize–winning literary giant. Samuel L. Jackson spent decades in minor roles before landing his breakthrough roles in *Jungle Fever* at forty-two and *Pulp Fiction* at forty-six. Julia Child didn't introduce the world to French cuisine until she was fifty, proving reinvention has no expiration date. Stan Lee cocreated Marvel's most legendary superheroes in his forties, reshaping pop culture forever. And Harland Sanders was nearly penniless until the franchising breakthrough at age sixty-five that led to KFC being one of the most recognized brands in the world. If they could do it, then why not me? Why not now? I mean, LeBron is still balling at forty years old.

The key is resilience: pushing through the noise and focusing on your own growth. I think about Kobe Bryant, whose work ethic was legendary. After missing key shots, he didn't wallow in defeat. He'd go back to the gym and take hundreds of shots, working on perfecting his craft. That kind of discipline is the difference between ordinary and extraordinary.

I used to think success was about chasing dreams as though the pursuit alone would bring fulfillment. But I've come to realize it's so much deeper than that. Success demands obsession—being enthralled, consumed, and deeply committed to the biggest ideals you hold for your life. You have to be a little crazy about yourself, to believe fiercely in possibilities that no one else can see, to create a vision so vivid that it pulls you forward when it would be easier to stop.

In solitary confinement, I started writing down everything I wanted to manifest in my life. I wrote myself an imaginary check with the amount I wanted to earn, envisioned the car I wanted to drive, and declared that I would become a bestselling author. I dared to dream bigger than my circumstances, bigger than the walls that confined me. And while it started as an exercise in hope, it became a practice of creation.

Today, I approach life the same way—with boldness, magic, and a sense of fun. I dream unapologetically and manifest relentlessly because I believe in the power of my vision, my imagination, and my ability to create the life I want. I've learned that to be a true dreamer and master manifester, you have to embrace your magic, lean into your "crazy," and, most importantly, enjoy the ride.

I have dream dates with my wife, where we sit up and dream together about what we want our lives to be. We go to open houses in the neighborhoods we desire to live in. We stay up watching videos of exotic cars, destinations, and places we want to travel to. We are intentional about the action boards we have in our heads. This isn't just about achieving goals—it's about living fully in the joy of possibility every single day.

I have also had to accept that failure is as much a part of the process as dreaming. The first time I was rejected during a sales pitch, I felt it deeply. But instead of letting it break me, I asked myself the hard questions: Was I being authentic? Did I do my best? The answer at the time was no, and from that moment on, I focused on improving, practicing, and honing my skills. Rejection is part of life, but the ability to push through it is a muscle you build.

Whenever I visit prisons now, I am reminded of how far I've come. Walking through those gates, hearing the heavy clank of the doors behind me, it's impossible not to reflect on my journey. I made it out, but so many people are still trapped—not just by the physical walls but by the mental prisons they've built for themselves. It's heartbreaking because I know those chains, the ones made of anger, shame, grief. During these visits, my purpose is to help people break free from those mental chains. Many don't believe they're worthy of freedom—whether it's literal freedom or freedom of the mind.

I've been there, stuck in that mindset of survival, believing that my past defined me. But once I shifted my focus, once I believed that success wasn't just possible but inevitable if I put in the work, everything began to change. Manifesting my dreams became a practice—writing them down, visualizing them with clarity, and speaking them into existence. Each step brought my goals closer not because of magic but because I had rooted them in a belief that felt unshakable. But the real magic? It started with forgiving myself and discovering my self-worth.

That sense of self-worth is the secret sauce, the foundation for developing the unshakable belief that fuels success. When you know you are worthy, everything shifts. You begin to see the universe as an ally rather than an obstacle. You trust that it is perfectly aligned with your deepest desires, that even the struggles and heartbreaks you've faced were uniquely designed to shape you into the ultimate version of yourself. As Marianne Williamson so eloquently stated, "Do not be afraid of your own greatness. You were born to stand out, not shrink into the shadows."

Self-worth unlocks a deeper understanding of self. It reminds you that you don't have to prove yourself to anyone. Instead, you work toward your dreams from a place of abundance and alignment, knowing that every experience—good or bad—has prepared you for this moment. When you truly believe you are worthy, you stop waiting for permission to succeed and start creating the life you were meant to live. That's when the magic really happens.

That's the power of belief. If you can see it, you can achieve it. But it's not just about seeing the goal—it's about being willing to do the work every single day.

Muhammad Ali didn't become the greatest by winning every fight. His greatest victories often came after crushing defeats. When he fought George Foreman, he spent eight rounds getting pummeled, but he stayed present. He waited for his moment, and then he struck. That's how life works—you have to stay patient because that opening will come. If you spend all your time focusing on how many times you've been knocked down, you'll never see the opportunity to rise. Stephen Curry, the greatest shooter to ever pick up a basketball, has made 3,822 three-pointers in his career—but he's also missed 5,151. That's more misses than most players will ever even attempt. And yet he keeps shooting. That's what makes him legendary—not just the shots he makes but the resilience to keep going, to take the next one no matter how many he's missed before. It's a reminder that greatness is about persistence, not perfection.

The people I meet in these prisons are often still trapped by their old stories and patterns. But it's not just those behind the bars of the thousands of prisons scattered across the world. I see it everywhere—people on the outside, living in hidden prisons of grief, anger, shame, and the inability to forgive.

But then there are those who are trapped in the hidden well-intentioned prisons—the ones that appear safe, even desirable, yet quietly erode the soul. The well-intentioned prisons of the helicopter parent who never lets go, the lover-turned-friend who stays out of comfort rather than love, the CEO who wears a mask of toughness because vulnerability feels like weakness, and the privileged child whose comfort breeds complacency.

So many bars, seen and unseen. So many hidden prisons, built in the mind and mistaken for freedom. But I'm living proof that you can break free, not just from the walls, but from the mental chains that keep you stuck in old cycles. My mission now is to help others find that freedom, to show them that there's a way out if they're willing to put in the work.

I know what it feels like to doubt yourself, to hear that voice in your head that tells you you're not good enough. I know what it feels like to be broken into pieces. But I've also learned how to silence that voice, put myself back together, and make deposits into my own narrative bank. We're quick to praise others, but we rarely do it for ourselves. But there is power in affirming oneself. That's why I challenge people to stand in front of the mirror and speak life into themselves. Because if you don't believe in your greatness, why should anyone else?

People like LeBron James or Muhammad Ali weren't arrogant when they proclaimed themselves as the greatest. They were simply acknowledging their own potential, their own magic. And that's what I've come to believe about myself. I didn't just survive—I thrived. I put in the work, disciplined my mind, and believed in my potential. Now my mission is to help others do the same, to find their unstoppable spirit and manifest the lives they deserve. Because the truth is, we're all capable of greatness. We just have to believe it.

Fearlessness isn't the absence of fear—it's the audacity to move forward despite it. It's about standing in the storm, unshaken, like Diana Ross in Central Park, drenched but undeterred. That image of resilience and grace reminds me that success is not about waiting for perfect conditions but about showing up, rain or shine, and owning your power.

Throughout my journey, I've learned that being unstoppable isn't about luck, talent, or even opportunity—it's about mindset, discipline, and the willingness to push past fear, doubt, and failure. It's about believing in yourself when no one else does. And it's about breaking free from the prisons—both real and imagined—that keep you from stepping into your greatness.

DIGGING DEEPER

Unstoppable spirits aren't born—they're forged through adversity, self-belief, and relentless action. When I look back at my journey, I recognize that my transformation wasn't just about escaping physical confinement but about freeing my mind from the limitations I had placed on myself.

The truth I've discovered is that unstoppable isn't a personality trait—it's a daily choice. It's choosing to show up when exhaustion tempts you to quit. It's choosing to believe in possibility when evidence suggests otherwise. It's choosing to take one more step forward when everything in you wants to retreat.

So I ask you, What would become possible if you decided, today, that your fears no longer get the final vote? What dreams have you shelved because they seemed too audacious? What gifts are you hiding because revealing them feels too vulnerable?

Your answers to these questions aren't just philosophical musings—they're the road map to your own unstoppable spirit. The distance between where you are and where you're meant to be isn't measured in miles or years but in the courage it takes to believe you're worthy of the journey.

🔑 KEYS TO BECOMING UNSTOPPABLE

1. Success Is Earned, Not Given
It's easy to look at successful people and assume they had it easier, but the truth is, success is the result of consistent, intentional effort over time. Just like Kobe Bryant, who spent hours in the gym after every missed shot, success belongs to those who show up every day and put in the work.

- Identify one area in your life where you need to be more disciplined.
- Set a small, measurable goal and commit to it daily (e.g., write five hundred words a day, practice your craft for an hour, network with one new person per week).

2. Master Your Mindset, Master Your Life
The biggest battle isn't external—it's the war in your own mind. Self-doubt, impostor syndrome, and limiting beliefs keep most people from reaching their full potential. But the difference between those who succeed and those who don't isn't talent—it's belief. When you tell yourself you are worthy, capable, and destined for more, your actions start to align with that truth.

- Engage in positive self-talk daily. Start each morning by looking in the mirror and affirming your power. Say, *I am worthy. I am capable. I am enough.*
- Rewire your beliefs. Write down the negative thoughts you struggle with. Next to each, write a new, empowering belief to replace it.

3. Fear Is a Compass, Not a Stop Sign
Fear isn't a signal to stop—it's a sign that you're stepping into something greater. The key is not to let fear paralyze you but to let it guide you. Every major leap in my life—from leaving Navan to stepping onto big stages—came with fear. But I did it anyway. Courage is action in the face of fear.

- List three things you've been avoiding due to fear.
- Take one small action toward each, even if it's just making a call, sending an email, or writing a plan.

4. Build a Support System That Elevates You

Success isn't a solo journey. Even the greats had a team—Jordan had Pippen, Ali had his trainers, and I have a network of friends, mentors, and supporters who challenge and uplift me. Surrounding yourself with people who believe in you is one of the most powerful success hacks.

- Identify three people who inspire and challenge you.
- Schedule a coffee, call, or check-in with one of them this week.

5. Manifestation Requires Action

Dreaming without action is just wishful thinking. I've always been a dreamer, but what made the difference was writing things down, visualizing them, and then doing the work to bring them to life. From making vision boards with my wife to attending open houses in our dream neighborhood, I learned that manifestation isn't magic—it's intention plus effort.

- Create a vision journal and write down your biggest dreams in vivid detail.
- Identify one concrete step you can take this week to move toward one of those dreams.

Every single person who has achieved greatness has had moments of doubt, fear, and failure. But what separates them from the rest is that they didn't stop. They kept going when it was hard, when it was lonely, when the odds were stacked against them.

You have that same power. You don't need permission to step into your greatness. You don't need validation to chase what sets your soul on fire. You just need the belief, the discipline, and the courage to take action—even when you're scared, even when the storm is raging.

Success isn't about waiting for the right moment. It's about becoming unstoppable in the face of whatever comes your way.

So the question is—are you ready to step into your power as the freest version of yourself?

CHAPTER THIRTEEN
FINDING TRUE FREEDOM

True freedom is impossible without a mind made free by discipline.

—Mortimer J. Adler

I was ten years old when I first heard Prince's "Free," and the lyrics have echoed in my mind ever since:

> Be glad that you are free
> Free to change your mind

At the time, I didn't fully understand the depth of those words. Freedom to a child feels simple—running outside without a curfew, exploring the world without boundaries. But as I grew older—especially after serving nineteen years in prison—my understanding of freedom evolved. I came to realize that real freedom has less to do with where you are and everything to do with how you feel inside.

These lyrics resonate so deeply with me because they capture what I've come to understand: Freedom isn't just a physical condition. You can be free from the bars of a prison but still be trapped in your mind. And you can walk around every day, not confined by walls yet still be imprisoned by fear, anger, grief, or shame. Freedom is a mental, emotional, and spiritual journey, and meditation on freedom is the gateway to your authentic self. It invites you to imagine a life unburdened by past grievances and fears.

Consider what your life would look like if you were truly free. How would you feel? Would you dance, smile, exercise, or laugh out loud? The reality is that you can do all those things right now. But you have to give up the prison of fear.

Fear of the unknown, of failure, of being found out, of embarrassment—these fears are deeply rooted in shame and keep us shackled to the narratives we've inherited or built around ourselves. Every time we replay an insult from the past, dwell on an experience where we felt slighted, or let someone else's judgment dictate our choices, we tighten the handcuffs around our wrists. We render ourselves powerless, locked in cycles of self-doubt and limitation.

True freedom begins the moment we confront these fears and make the choice to live differently. It's about recognizing the layers of fear that society, upbringing, and insecurities have piled onto us: the fear of aging in a culture that idolizes youth and marginalizes the wisdom and beauty of growing older; the fear of other people's narrow worldviews, as if their limited perspectives somehow diminish our truth; the fear of not being enough—smart enough, attractive enough, wealthy enough—or of being unworthy of love and acceptance. These fears, so pervasive and insidious, convince us to play small, to hide, to defer our dreams, and to live by someone else's rules.

But freedom doesn't come from avoiding fear; it comes from acknowledging it and refusing to let it dictate our lives. It's learning to see the cracks in those fears, the light that seeps through when we choose courage over comfort. It's reminding ourselves that fear is often a reflection of what we care about most and that stepping through it is how we claim our power. Whether it's the fear of failing at something new, the fear of aging, or the fear of not living up to expectations, freedom lies in embracing those fears and choosing to move forward anyway.

Living differently means rewriting the stories fear has written for us and stepping boldly into the unknown. It means showing up as our authentic selves, with all our imperfections and vulnerabilities, and understanding that true worth is found not in external validation but in the courage to be free from the chains of shame and judgment. Only then can we begin to live fully, unapologetically, and without limits.

I will never forget the excitement that washed over me as a kid watching an old film about the world's greatest escape artist, Harry Houdini. It was mesmerizing watching him free himself from what seemed like impossible situations—handcuffs, straitjackets, even tanks filled with water. Later, I was captivated by the feats of David Copperfield, with his escape from Alcatraz, and by David Blaine's frozen-in-time event, where he was encased in a block of ice for sixty-three hours. These men weren't just magicians; they were escape artists who dared to defy the odds. They didn't just escape; they made us believe that the impossible could be possible.

I wasn't a magician, but life demanded that I become an escape artist of my own kind. My stage wasn't lit with bright lights, and there were no crowds holding their breath as I worked. My acts of escape were quiet, unseen, and deeply personal. The stakes, however, were just as high—my freedom, my survival, and ultimately, my life.

One of my prisons was physical, with real bars, real locks, and real walls. But as confining as that space was, it wasn't nearly as powerful as the mental prisons I discovered while serving time. The cell I lived in for years was tangible, but the ones in my mind were insidious, hidden, and far more difficult to escape.

These mental prisons took many forms: the narratives I had been told about myself, the guilt and shame that played on repeat, and the belief that my circumstances defined my worth. These invisible walls felt so real, they almost had the verisimilitude of freedom. Almost.

But it wasn't just about my own prisons—I came to realize that we are all trapped in one way or another. For many of us, these prisons aren't as obvious as steel bars. They're the relentless churn of the news cycle, designed to keep us in a state of fear and anxiety. They're the FOMO (fear of missing out) that drives us to compare our lives to curated versions of success we see online.

They're the endless doom scrolling, feeding us despair one swipe at a time.

Then there are the deeper, more personal prisons: Comparing our lives to those of celebrities and influencers who make their perfection seem effortless. The pain of a marred childhood that we carry like an invisible weight. The toxic relationships we cling to out of fear or habit. And even the cultural mindset of entitlement, which traps us in a cycle of discontent, always wanting more but never feeling enough.

Escaping these prisons requires more than just awareness; it demands intention, effort, and a willingness to confront uncomfortable truths. Like Houdini studying every lock and mechanism, I had to develop an acuity for spotting the traps in my thinking, the patterns that kept me stuck. It required perspicacious self-awareness to discern what was holding me back and the courage to believe that I could break free.

In the process, I became a raconteur of my own freedom, rewriting the story of my life with each escape. Every time I slipped out of a limiting belief or freed myself from the weight of the past, I added a new chapter to the tale. Escaping wasn't just about getting out—it was about building something better on the other side.

What I've learned is that the art of escaping isn't about brute force or luck. It's about strategy, mindset, and determination. It's about recognizing the prisons we're in, no matter how subtle or normalized they might seem, and finding a way to slip free—not through rebellion or destruction but through clarity and intention.

Life's prisons may look different for each of us, but the path to freedom is universal. It starts with this simple truth: The key isn't out there—it's within you. You just have to find it. And when you do, you'll discover that freedom isn't just the absence of confinement. It's the presence of possibility.

Because the greatest escape isn't just about getting out. It's about breaking through to a life that's truly yours.

The Ecosystem of Freedom

Freedom is like an ecosystem. It requires balance: owning our truth, being accountable to it, speaking it, creating space for it, and living it. But when the ecosystem is out of balance, we risk lashing out, avoiding healthy relationships, fighting ghosts, resisting love, or reimprisoning ourselves. Mindfulness brings you back to the moment of truth, reminding you that the only freedom that exists is in the now—not in yesterday or tomorrow.

Our most valuable asset is time. Once it's gone, we can't get it back, so it's crucial to value it today and maximize each moment's potential. A free life must include joy—both spontaneous and intentional. A life without joy is broken and filled with sorrow.

Setting a Freedom Date

One of the most powerful steps toward freedom is setting a "freedom date." This is the day you commit to liberating yourself from the mental and emotional prisons you've built. Just like counting down the days in confinement, you need to set a future date that signifies your new beginning, your separation from the past. Write it down—on a piece of paper, in your journal, or even in the margins of this book. Set it in stone in your mind and don't move it for anyone. When that day comes, dress in your best outfit and go out into the world as if you've just been released from a long sentence. Live it up to the fullest and bask in the freedom you achieved.

The Journey of Self-Discovery and Healing

My journey toward freedom started when I realized I was incarcerated long before I entered prison, and I was free long before my release. Through journaling, mindfulness, and meditation, I unlocked the mental bars that had held me back since childhood. From there, it has been one step at a time—sometimes with a sidestep or two. This process led me to several truths:

1. My authentic self is both amazing and deserving of amazing things.
2. Ultimate freedom is expressed through dominion over my own thoughts.
3. Manifestation requires constant patience and practice.
4. Obstacles are part of the journey. Growth comes from using the keys within us to unlock the doors in front of us.

It took a lot of journaling, meditation, and giving up the old narratives that had kept me imprisoned. But freedom comes with the understanding that the old narratives don't go away easily; they fight to stick around. Twenty years ago, I wrote this in my journal, and it still applies to this day:

Journal Entry: May 31, 2005

It's been over a year since I've been out of the hole and just as long since I last wrote in my journal. A lot has changed in that time. One of the most significant changes is that I've become much more aware of myself. Through writing, I've learned to see myself clearly.

I've made progress in controlling my anger, though there are still moments when I feel vexed. The difference now is that I have a greater desire—and ability—to control my response to the things that upset me. This shift has been transformative, helping me maintain my focus and stay grounded.

Though I am out of prison, the stories I told myself at my lowest point come up from time to time, but now I can combat them a lot easier.

Resurrecting the Artist Within

For me, freedom is deeply tied to creativity and imagination. I had to resurrect the artist within myself, embracing the language of freedom, which includes liberty, dreaming, visualization, audaciousness, and activation. Writing became my way of unleashing my subconscious, birthing something meaningful into the world. Although I once dreamed of being a visual artist, I learned to paint pictures with words, inspired by the golden era of hip-hop artists like Rakim, Scarface, KRS-One, and Ice Cube, who depicted inner-city life with such vivid storytelling.

Through this journey, I also rediscovered the thing that sets my soul on fire—fiction writing. I've spent years writing, speaking, and coaching, but the part of me that dreams wildly and tells stories is ready to take center stage. This is the next chapter of my creative journey—bringing my fiction to the world.

In solitary confinement, after I wrote the text that would become my first book and was cursed out by a man in a cell a few doors down, I developed some apprehension about sharing my writing. The sting of rejection, even from another incarcerated man, made me question whether my words were worth putting into the world. But once I got out of solitary and started sharing my work, the response was overwhelmingly positive. Word spread through the cell block, and soon, I had to create a sign-up list just so men could take turns reading my books—books that I had written by hand, in the quiet of my confinement, unsure if they would ever mean anything to anyone but me.

That experience taught me something: The fear of sharing is universal, but so is the power of connection. It made me think about the greats—how many of them almost let their doubts keep them from releasing their work.

Maya Angelou struggled with sharing her voice. Trauma silenced her for years, and even as she wrote *I Know Why the Caged Bird Sings*, she feared how the world would react. But she shared it anyway, and in doing so, she gave countless others the courage to tell their own stories.

Tyler, the Creator was laughed at for his music. Industry insiders dismissed him as too weird, too different. But instead of changing to fit their mold, he built his own lane, creating music for the people who *did* get it. Now those same people who doubted him watch as he headlines festivals and wins Grammys.

Vincent van Gogh painted in obscurity, never knowing if his work would matter. He only sold one painting in his lifetime. Imagine if he had stopped. Imagine if he had let his fears keep him from creating. Today, his art is priceless, his name immortal.

And then there's me. Sitting in a prison cell, wondering if my words mattered. But I pushed past the fear, shared anyway, and saw how stories—my stories—could move people, even in the darkest of places.

The truth is, every artist, every creator, every visionary has been afraid to share their work. But the ones who change the world are the ones who do it anyway.

Once I awakened the artist within, writing became my lifeline. It gave my life meaning and purpose, helping me realize that it's never too late to pursue your passions, no matter how outdated or out of touch they may seem. So what's stopping you?

Living in the Now

The only freedom that exists is in the now. Freedom thinking shifts everything inside of you. It reveals a lightness in your step, a brightness in your smile—you are in your essence. It's a state where you are not just free from external constraints but liberated from the internal ones that keep you from living fully. You don't have to wait until society says you are fit or the parole board says you are ready. You can escape at this very moment, without fear of being shot down by a guard or caught in concertina wire. But you have to make the choice to stay or go. Now take some time out today and lean into this powerful meditation.

Meditation on Freedom in the Now

Find a quiet space. Sit comfortably. Close your eyes. Take a deep breath in . . . hold it for a moment . . . and exhale slowly.

Inhale . . . feel the air expand within you.

Exhale . . . release anything that feels heavy.

Let yourself settle into this moment. Right here. Right now.

The Present Is Where Freedom Lives

The only freedom that exists is in the now—not in the past that lingers behind you, not in the future that hasn't arrived. Freedom is here, in this breath, in this stillness.

Feel your body relax as you step fully into this moment.

Feel the weight of old regrets, past hurts, and unspoken fears begin to loosen.

They do not belong to you right now. They only exist if you hold on to them.

Breathe in lightness—a step unburdened.

Breathe out heaviness—all that you no longer need.

The Choice to Be Free

In this space, you are not trapped. You are not waiting.

You do not need permission to be free.

No external force can hold you. Freedom is an internal decision.

Picture yourself standing before two doors—one is labeled "Stay," the other "Go."

This is your choice.

The door of the past may call to you—memories, regrets, old narratives of who you were.

But you hold the key. You can lock that door if it no longer serves you.

Or perhaps there is a part of you still held hostage—an old fear, a painful experience, a version of yourself that longs to be released. If you are ready, unlock that door. Free them. Free yourself.

Freedom Thinking Shifts Everything

Breathe in and feel the lightness in your body.

Breathe out and let go of anything that no longer aligns with the person you are becoming.

Freedom is a state of mind. It is not earned. It is claimed.

And you, right now, are claiming it.

Returning to the Present

Slowly bring your awareness back to your breath. Feel the space around you.

Know that you are free—not someday, not when circumstances change, but right now.

Take this freedom with you. Walk with it. Speak with it. Live from it.

When you are ready, open your eyes.

You are free. You have always been free. And now you know it.

Creating Your Freedom Blueprint

To truly embrace freedom, we must design our own freedom ecosystem. This includes setting freedom boundaries, defining the things that protect our freedom, and creating personal mantras that reinforce our liberated state.

Here is an example of what that mantra can look like for you:

I don't have to wait to be free. I am free right now.

I am free from the weight of my past.

I don't owe my old mistakes my future.

I don't carry the baggage of shame, guilt, or regret.

They don't define me—I do.

Whether it's a freedom checklist, a freedom manual, or a freedom journal, the goal is to build a personal blueprint that guides you toward a life of agency, empowerment, and fulfillment.

Ultimately, freedom is about gratitude. The greatest expression of freedom is trusting that the moment you're in is divine and worthy of your presence. Be thankful for this very moment, this very freedom, and the choice you made to liberate yourself.

The Basement of Fear: Confronting Hidden Traumas

I hated the basement of our childhood home; I imagined it filled with creeps who were waiting for me to descend the stairs. No matter how many times I had to go down to that cellar, I couldn't shake my anxiety—even though those monsters never materialized. We all have basements in our minds where fears reside. To grow, we must venture into these dark spaces, confront the hidden fears, and expose real trauma to the light.

Manifestation: Trusting the Creator's Promise

Manifestation is the process of trusting the Creator's promise and having faith that the universe is aligning in your favor. It's like holding on to the belief that the Creator's plan is unfolding as it should, even when the road is unclear. This belief in manifestation is akin to planting seeds without knowing exactly when they'll sprout but trusting that the bloom will come.

The Courage to Be Free

When I first sat down to write this book, I had no idea how much more liberated I would feel by the end of it. Writing has always been my tool for transformation, but this process forced me to confront my own limitations and take action in ways I hadn't before.

One of the biggest steps I took was finally applying for my pardon. For years, I carried the weight of my past—grieving the time lost to prison, feeling the sting of having to check "Yes" every time I was asked if I had been convicted of a crime, and battling the shame when my past affected my family. I was tired of it. So instead of just sitting with frustration, I did something about it. I set aside time, downloaded the application, filled it out, and submitted it.

It's been months since I sent it off, and I still don't have an answer. But here's the thing—I already feel lighter. Not because someone granted me permission to move forward but because I took ownership of my own freedom.

And that's the lesson I want to leave you with: Freedom isn't something we wait for. It's something we claim.

Embracing the Next Chapter

Today, I sit in a spirit of gratitude.

I am grateful for Sherrod and Indy and the impact they've had on my life.

I am grateful for Sekou's resilience—how he's taking control of his health with a strength that humbles me. Watching him administer his own insulin shots still blows my mind—and sometimes brings me to tears. But more than anything, I am proud of him.

I am grateful for the joyful moments I share with my wife, Liz, dreaming and imagining the next phase of our lives together.

But gratitude doesn't just sit in my mind—it pushes me into action. To be clear, journaling, meditation, creating an action board, and creating a mantra are not passive exercises. It's not some set-it-and-forget-it process. If you're doing it right, if you're sitting with your truth, it will force you to take action. It will force you to get off your ass and grab life by the reins.

Because here's the truth:

It doesn't have to be perfect. But it does have to be a process. It has to be progress.

You Were Not Put Here to Play Small

In the past, I had to ask myself hard questions: Why am I so comfortable in pain and chaos? Why does peace scare me so much?

The answer? Because I had grown accustomed to the abnormal being normal. For so long, I equated struggle with survival, with identity, with meaning. But once I called that out, I began the arduous journey of steadying myself in peace. Of allowing myself to live in joy without waiting for the other shoe to drop.

This is the work of freedom thinking.

This is the work of becoming whole.

This is the work of owning your space in the world.

Start Before You're Ready

When I first started writing, I had no idea what I was doing. All I knew was that I loved words. My grasp of punctuation was basic at best—I could handle a question mark, a period, an exclamation point, but semicolons and colons? That was a different story. But I didn't let what I didn't know stop me.

During my incarceration, I devoured books—nearly fifteen hundred of them. Westerns, mysteries, horror, self-help, philosophy—you name it. But despite all that reading, I wasn't a trained writer. I wasn't an MFA graduate, a grammar expert, or a punctuation specialist. None of the traditional markers of a "writer" applied to me.

Still, I wrote. I tried.

I put pen to paper and let the stories take shape. And in the process, I realized that success isn't about waiting until you're ready—it's about starting. It's about giving yourself permission to do the work.

That applies to anything—writing, speaking, entrepreneurship, relationships. You don't need someone to tell you you're qualified. You don't need the perfect degree, the right connections, or a permission slip.

What you need is the willingness to begin.

Friendship, Purpose, and the Power of Showing Up

Finding your purpose is one of the most important things you can do. But here's what I've learned:

Purpose isn't a finish line—it's a practice.

It's something you pursue daily, through the choices you make, the people you surround yourself with, and the way you show up in the world.

And let's be clear—friendship matters.

Not the surface-level kind. Not the "I'll hit you up when I need something" kind. Real friendship. The kind that sharpens you, holds you accountable, and reminds you of who the hell you are when you forget.

If you have those people in your life, cherish them. And if you don't—go find them.

Because the truth is, none of us were meant to do this alone.

Your Freedom, Your Choice

As I close this book, I want to leave you with this:

You were not placed in the arena, in these big rooms, in these powerful spaces to play small.

You were not given the gift of thought, creativity, and vision just to sit on the sidelines.

You don't have to wait until society decides you are fit.

You don't have to wait until the parole board says you're ready.

You don't have to wait until the world gives you permission to be free.

You can claim your freedom—right now.

Right here.

At this very moment.

The only question is, Are you going to take it?

Let's get free.

Recommendations

Books

The Artist's Way by Julia Cameron

The Art of War by Sun Tzu

The Art of Worldly Wisdom by Baltasar Gracián

As a Man Thinketh by James Allen

Atomic Habits by James Clear

Daring Greatly by Brené Brown

The Hard Thing About Hard Things by Ben Horowitz

I Know Why the Caged Bird Sings by Maya Angelou

Long Walk to Freedom by Nelson Mandela

Man's Search for Meaning by Viktor E. Frankl

The Miracle of Mindfulness: An Introduction to the Practice of Meditation by Thich Nhat Hanh

Thick Face, Black Heart by Chin-Ning Chu

This Is Strategy by Seth Godin

Tuesdays with Morrie by Mitch Albom

What Happened to You? by Dr. Bruce Perry and Oprah Winfrey

RECOMMENDATIONS

You²: A High-Velocity Formula for Multiplying Your Personal Effectiveness in Quantum Leaps by Price Pritchett

Podcasts

All the Smoke

The Ben & Marc Show

Deeply Well with Devi Brown

KG Certified

The Mel Robbins Podcast

The Oprah Podcast

Pivot

The Rich Roll Podcast

The School of Greatness

The Tim Ferriss Show

The Tony Robbins Podcast

Playlist

"Black Butterfly" by Deniece Williams

"Blessings" by Big Sean

"Composure" by Nas featuring Hit-Boy (and yours truly)

"Dream On" by Aerosmith

"Feel" by Kendrick Lamar

RECOMMENDATIONS

"Free" by Prince

"God Did" by DJ Khaled featuring Rick Ross, Lil Wayne, Jay-Z, John Legend, and Fridayy

"If I Ruled the World (Imagine That)" by Nas featuring Lauryn Hill

"Maggot Brain" by Funkadelic

"My First Song" by Jay-Z

"My Way" by Frank Sinatra

"Paid in Full" by Eric B. and Rakim

"Sailing" by Christopher Cross

"Simply Beautiful" by Al Green

"The Way I Am" by Eminem

"Yebba's Heartbreak" by Drake and Yebba

"Zoom" by the Commodores

Acknowledgments

This book—and the journey that led to it—wouldn't exist without the people who've poured into me, walked beside me, and lifted me when I needed it most.

Over the last fifteen years of freedom, I've learned that liberation isn't just the absence of bars—it's the presence of love, belief, and unwavering support. I am where I am today because so many of you saw something in me before the world did. You leaned in to speak my name in rooms I'd never stepped foot in. You listened with your eyes, read between the lines of my earliest work, and felt the truth I was still learning how to tell.

You've shown me what it means to be seen, to be championed, and to be loved through evolution. Your support didn't just elevate my career—it helped me rediscover my humanity. You've shaped my life in ways far beyond these pages, and I carry your impact with deep, enduring gratitude.

To my wife, Liz—thank you for being my peace, my compass, my sounding board, and my sanctuary. Your belief in me is the soil where everything I do grows. Thank you for being a mirror of love, devotion, and commitment to shared dreams.

To Sekou, my son—you've been patient when I've been hunkered down working on this book, and you've cheered me on as

ACKNOWLEDGMENTS

only a son can. You remind me daily of what resilience looks like and what joy feels like.

To my oldest son, Jay—distance and miles can never separate the love I hold in my heart for you.

To my parents and in-laws—James White, Marie White, Arlene Howard, and Pat and Nate Dozier and in loving memory of Ron Howard—thank you for the love, the lessons, and the sacrifices that paved the way for Liz and me to start our own family legacy.

To my siblings—Alan, Art, Tamica, Will (Kidd), Vanessa, Nakia, Jason E. Howard, Shamica Bootsy, and the spirit of Sherrod—you remind me of my roots, my resilience, and my responsibility. I carry all of you with me, always. To my sister-in-law, Mary Dozier—thank you for being a dope little sister and addition to our family.

To Ben Horowitz—thank you for being the dopest, rawest, and realest friend and brother. To Felicia Horowitz—thank you for being a light and clarifying force in my life. I appreciate you, big sis!

To Deron and June—your friendship has been a divine spark. A single dinner conversation turned into this book-publishing experience—that's the power of alignment, timing, and real connection.

To my brothers Cal, Fame, Datwon, and QDIII—thank you for the inspiration. Your insight and creativity push me to think bigger while staying grounded.

To my CAA family—Michelle Kydd Lee, my agent Cait Hoyt, and my dear brother Carlos Segarra—thank you for helping bring this book into the world through your relentless efforts and for

ACKNOWLEDGMENTS

challenging me to be the best. To Peter Jacobs, Inez Maza, and Josh Lingren—looking forward to taking the world by storm with you.

To my CAA Foundation crew, Deborah Marcus, Natalie Tran, and Callie Rivers—thank you for the meaningful work you do to make the world a better place!

To my Authors Equity (AE) dream team—Madeline McIntosh, Nina von Moltke, Don Weisberg, Andrea Bachofen, Carly Gorga, Craig Young, Ilana Gold, Deb Lewis, Rose Edwards, Sarah Christensen Fu, and JoliAmour Dubose-Morris—you moved mountains, believed in me, and helped me aim higher than I thought possible. I truly hope that other authors get this lucky! LGF! To James Clear—thank you for your brilliance and the generosity of time and wisdom you have shared. Happy to be on this journey with you!

I am eternally grateful for my Navan (TripActions) colleagues, both current and former—Ariel Cohen, Ilan Twiggs, Rich Liu, Michael Sindich, Grant McGrail, Kelly Soderland, Ofer Ben-David, and Nina Herold—and every leader building something that reshapes the world of travel and expenses. You've shown me what innovation and leadership look like when rooted in purpose.

To Carlos Delatorre, Sai Jahann, Danny Finkel, and Thomas Tuchescherer—those countless conversations still echo. Thank you for being part of my early path.

To my large and hilarious extended family, the White, Neal, Davis, and O'Neal families—your collective love and laughter are cherished gifts. Special shout-out to my Aunt Bernadette—thank you for being the heart of that love. And big shout-out to my cousin, lil bro Jerrel—it's up!

ACKNOWLEDGMENTS

Love and gratitude to Nana, Sophia, Mariah, Jules, and the Horowitz tribe—your support means the world to me.

To Chris Lyons, Meghan Alexander, Stacia Murray, Kofi Ampadu, and the A16Z family, along with the CLF and TXO teams—you inspire me to stand tall in my purpose. Thank you for modeling excellence, courage, and care.

To Nas, Hit-Boy, art and impact, legacy and sound—thank you for including me in one of the greatest hip-hop collaborations of all time, *King's Disease II*.

To Brad Keywell and Emily Slade—thank you for being incredibly inspiring collaborators on Street Philosophy Society! I am so proud to go on this journey with you!

To my dear friends, collaborators, and conspirators for good, Adrienne Alexander, Chloe, Maud and Tad Arnold, Shawn Wilson, Trabian Shorters, Tonya Allen, Dr. Bob Ross, and the entire BMe Community and Soar—thank you.

To my Wasatch family—you believed in me early, and our time together is meaningful and enriching. I'm grateful.

To Reid Hoffman and Michelle Yee—thank you for always having my back. To Jess Sousa, Colin Raney, Sean Bonner, and Joi Ito—you've each been a light in different moments of this journey. I'm thankful for every one of you and what you have meant in my life.

To Chris Collins, my coach and brother in screenwriting—thank you for being a man of your word and for all the dope sessions. To my peeps Kristin Jones, Arielle Vavasseur, and Natalie Benjamin at Inside Projects—one thing for sure is the Queens always come through for Kings! This work wouldn't be the same without you.

ACKNOWLEDGMENTS

To the Paid in Full Foundation—thank you for believing and investing in the legacy of the greats. Your vision is changing lives. To Divine, Michelle Ebanks, Judy Smith, Fab Five Freddy, and Steve Stoute—salute and love!

Much love and respect to the Virginia Tech LIT Crew. Thank you for reigniting the conversation on the importance of the humanities in leadership. Thank you to my freedom fighters, Ashley Lucas, Jessica Jackson, Prisoner Creative Arts Project (PCAP), Anti-Recidivism Coalition (ARC) Reform Alliance, and everyone who works on behalf of people in prison.

To Moonshot—Lauren, Ryan, Joel, and Sandy—your creativity, belief, and magic helped me imagine the impossible and make it real across so many dope projects. Thank you for walking this dream into the light with me.

To my incredible cover designer, Pete Garceau—you are a creative and brilliant design wizard. Thank you!

Lastly, I want to take a special moment and space to thank my editor, Megan Newman. Thank you for coming out of retirement to go on this journey with me. You helped me clarify the stories and find the lessons I desired to share. You showed up with your full humanity and heart on display, and I am truly honored that you chose me and this manuscript. All love and respect!

Detroit raised me. LA embraced me. I carry both cities in my heart—steel and sunshine, grit and dreams!

LGF (Let's Get Free).

Shaka

About the Author

Shaka Senghor is an inspirational speaker, entrepreneur, and author of the New York Times bestselling books *Writing My Wrongs* and *Letters to the Sons of Society*. A sought-after resilience expert and recognized "Soul Igniter" in Oprah Winfrey's inaugural Super Soul 100, Senghor has captivated and transformed global audiences with his extraordinary journey from incarceration to influence. Through raw authenticity and profound insight, he doesn't just share his story—he equips others with the exact resilience practices that fueled his own remarkable transformation, proving that reinvention isn't just possible—it's within everyone's reach.

Continue on Your Freedom Journey

Thank you so much for walking this path with me through *How to Be Free*. This work isn't just words on pages—it's the blueprint that transformed my life from confinement to liberation, and I'm deeply honored to have shared it with you.

If these pages have sparked something within you and you want to continue your journey toward freedom, I invite you to join my weekly newsletter, Hidden Prisons.

Each week you'll receive

- a powerful quote that challenges conventional thinking,
- my personal insights that unpack deeper truths, and
- a specific, actionable step to dismantle whatever barriers are holding you back.

Transform your mindset and unlock your potential in just five minutes a week.

You can sign up at shakasenghor.com/newsletter.

Let's get free.